A collection of children's writing
from the 2004 awards.

UNIVERSITY PRESS

OXFORD
UNIVERSITY PRESS

Great Clarendon Street, Oxford OX2 6DP

Oxford University Press is a department of the University of Oxford.
It furthers the University's objective of excellence in research, scholarship,
and education by publishing worldwide in
Oxford New York
Auckland Cape Town Dar es Salaam Hong Kong Karachi
Kuala Lumpur Madrid Melbourne Mexico City Nairobi
New Delhi Shanghai Taipei Toronto

With offices in
Argentina Austria Brazil Chile Czech Republic France Greece
Guatemala Hungary Italy Japan South Korea Poland Portugal
Singapore Switzerland Thailand Turkey Ukraine Vietnam

First published 2004

British Library Cataloguing in Publication Data
Data available

ISBN 0 19 834959 9

1 3 5 7 9 10 8 6 4 2

Illustrations by Jess Mikhail

Typeset by Palimpsest Book Production Limited, Polmont, Stirlingshire

Printed in Great Britain by Cox and Wyman, Ltd, Berkshire

The events in these texts are fictitious, and any resemblance to events
is purely coincidental. The opinions expressed are not
those of the awards organiser or the publisher.

MENCAP Understanding Learning Disability: Charity Registration No 222377

# CONTENTS

FOREWORD

Stephen Twigg MP
Minister for Schools

Welcome to the Write Here, Write Now 2004 book of winning entries, written by children for children.

The Write Here, Write Now writing awards encourage children aged 8–10 to be creative and to have fun with writing. The awards support the commitment in the Primary National Strategy to improve children's writing skills and promote their enjoyment of writing. Combining excellence in teaching with enjoyment of learning is at the heart of the Strategy. We recognise the importance of developing children's learning skills to the full whilst making their learning a rich and enjoyable experience. We have seen year on year improvement in the richness of words and creativity of imagination applied in writing.

Write Here, Write Now 2004 has been very successful and received 29,412 entries from across England. I very much appreciate the support from writers Gillian Cross, Brian Patten, Nick Arnold and Lizo Mzimba who provided advice and opening lines for children to continue. Thank you for helping to excite and engage children's imaginations and for inspiring them to write some excellent pieces of work. There were many high quality entries which showed great creativity and originality and which were enjoyable to read.

I would also like to thank the judges and all the teachers who supported the awards. But, most of all, my thanks go to all the children who took part.

Stephen Twigg

INTRODUCTION

The Write Here, Write Now national writing awards for primary schools are run by the Department for Education and Skills. The breadth and originality of the entries received from 8–10 year-olds reveal a wealth of budding writers around the country.

Children had four categories to choose from: Poem, Persuasive writing, Story and, for group entries, Journalism. In the Poem category, **Brian Patten's** opening lines encouraged children to think about something 'unique and fabulous' behind the door. **Nick Arnold** asked children to consider whether science is our friend or our enemy. **Gillian Cross'** opening piece for the Story category inspired imaginative and thrilling journeys into the world of Captain Joshua Wright's telescope. Groups entering the Journalism category followed advice from BBC *Newsround's* **Lizo Mzimba** to write a TV or newspaper report based on their choice from three pictures.

From the huge number of entries received, regional winners were chosen at judging sessions around the country. The national winners were selected by a panel of experts, including the well-known writers above. In addition to the regional and national winners, there are the winners of the Improvement Awards, nominated by their teachers for making significant progress with their writing.

The children's ages given are those at the time of writing their entries. Their work has been lightly edited to keep their individual styles.

POEM

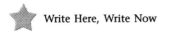

Brian Patten wrote . . .

When we opened the door yesterday
Beyond it we found
Something unique and fabulous
That left us spellbound . . .

Introducing the poems

Brian Patten's introduction encouraged young writers to visualise something unique and fabulous. The winning pieces take us to a wide range of imaginative situations with vivid, colourful descriptions of people, animals, aliens and events. Some are funny, others poignant – they all draw us in to experience what's beyond the open door.

A haunting atmosphere is created by **Olivia Merrett** in an ambitious poem about a tragic event.

Eloise Lombard's clever poem has a comical style. Find out what happens when an alien comes to visit.

A unique perspective of the world is created in **James Kelly's** poem, which is enhanced by his use of words and rhymes.

Becca Killen's poem is an inventive and personal account about receiving a special gift.

Powerful emotions about a close family member are conveyed in **Emily Ashworth's** poem through her careful handling of language and structure.

Qasim Khalil uses rich and powerful language to describe an extraordinary creature he finds on the other side of the door. What could it be?

Catherine Regan gives a very inventive description of a sweet-eater's paradise – but is it all too much?

Imagery is used to full effect in **Joseph Bridgland's** poem about a night-time journey. His evocative words build a sense of excitement.

Katie Legg's very visual and fun poem describes a neighbour's pet who is behaving in a very odd way.

Katherine Burdon uses wonderful imagery to create a moving poem about a journey into a majestic new world.

Calum Wickham's fun poem describes a weird world he discovers behind a magical door. What does he see?

The Ship of Dreams

A portal back to Titanic times
The ghosts of unforgotten past
There they will dance to the end of time
Due to the iceberg that killed the last.

A time of unique life
A world with no fear
No time to worry
Titanic is here.

My feelings are of guilt
For the people who lost their lives
The ship that was said to be magically built.

On Titanic we stayed
With people who went low
Titanic, the ship of dreams.

When we opened the door yesterday, or was it long ago?

By Olivia Merrett, aged 9
South Petherton Junior School

SOUTH WEST WINNER

The Martian who came for Tea

It hopped up on that table
It sat down on a chair
It ate up all our cornflakes
'Till there were hardly any there!

This Martian had an appetite
And it was clear to see
This Martian who was hungry
Was gobbling all our tea!

It swallowed all the apple juice
It begged for more and more
It didn't seem to like the eggs
And dropped them on the floor!

It raided all the drawers
Hunting for more food
We had nothing left downstairs
And he became rather rude!

Then it went upstairs
And searched my secret stash
Those sweets were expensive
I'd spent all my cash!

When it had finished and it was full
It finally went home
The fact it ate my mum and dad
Left me all alone.

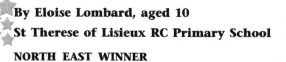By Eloise Lombard, aged 10
St Therese of Lisieux RC Primary School

NORTH EAST WINNER

The World Which Was Upside Down!!!

I opened the door
And what did I see?
The pigs and the badgers
Up high in the tree.

The birds on the ground
The cat in the sky
The cow on the wall
And some passers-by.

The car on the roof
With an engine on top
It was going so fast
It gave me a shock.

When I glanced all around
I saw filled with surprise
The world was upside down
In front of my eyes.

The fish in the grass,
The dogs in the pond
The goats in their beds
And what was beyond?

The Sun and the Moon
Were down on the ground,
These were the things
That left me spellbound!

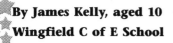 By James Kelly, aged 10

Wingfield C of E School

IMPROVEMENT AWARDS JOINT WINNER

The Golden Quad Bike

It was a golden quad bike with a black leather seat.

When I sit upon my quad bike,
With my helmet on
There are pads on my knees and arms
And a jacket with a number one.

I can go faster and faster,
Round and round the track.
Making sure I don't hit anything
Before I get back.

With the wind on my face,
And my shiny goggles on.
I ride to and fro
Until my sad is gone.

Now I am happy and smiling,
With lots of energy left.
I think I will polish my quad bike
And hide it against theft.

By Becca Killen, aged 10
Hexham Middle School

IMPROVEMENT AWARDS JOINT WINNER

The Photo

With two sets of eyes
Staring happily,
One set was Grandad's
The others belonged to me.

Seeing his smile
And his cheery face,
Warms up my heart
With a loving embrace.

I looked at the photo
For hours on end,
Looking at Grandad,
To remember-pretend.

I dream he is here
Smiling again,
Holding the memory
Was driving me insane.

I know you are near
My loving heart wished,
Your life may have ended
But not finished!

Two sets of eyes
Staring up at me,
One set was Grandad's
The others belonged to me.

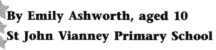**By Emily Ashworth, aged 10**
St John Vianney Primary School

NORTH WEST WINNER

The Phoenix

Incredible and most unique
Fabulous was the word
Something to inspire
Nothing like you would have seen
Before

Wings of sunlight
As bright as the sun
As colourful as a rainbow

Where ever it goes brightness appears
Even though you fly all around the
World
What is its name?
Beauty is the true word

What beauty of flames?
Ashes burning high and low
What could it be?
So much to admire
Glamorous and splendid creature

Creator of all, what is this?
Bird of architecture
Disappear this silence
Tell me what you are?

Speak out loud,
Tell me what people name you?

Open your mouth
Wide and tell me
Fade this silence
Tell me!

"I am the phoenix!
I'll burn through the door."

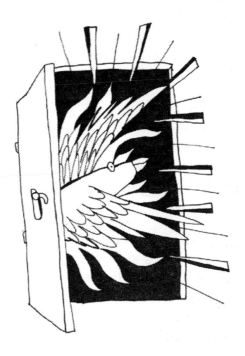

By Qasim Khalil, aged 10
Parkinson Lane Primary Community School
YORKSHIRE AND THE HUMBER WINNER

Chocolate Glory

A garden of chocolate and colourful sweets,
A smell that tempted me on.
The candyfloss leaves on the sugar plum trees,
That tasted of lemon bon-bon.

The jelly baby bush that had a hundred flavours
From cool mint to strawberry cream.
A lovely smell of melting toffee
I hope it's not a dream.

A sugar candy nest rests in a tree
With chocolate eggs inside,
As each one cracks a fluffy chick
Breaks free and runs to hide.

Butter icing petals on sponge cake flowers
That taste like they've just been cooked.
I wish I could stay here for hours and hours,
This place has got me hooked.

I dip my fingers in sherbet pollen
It made my tongue tickle so.
Angelica grass and butter buttercups,
Jelly beans row upon row.

A sweety eater's paradise,
A chocolate lover's dream
A truly scrumptious menu,
A parlour of ice-cream.

Some cherry lips to nibble
Or a lolly to lick
Oh me . . . Oh my . . .
I'm starting to feel sick!!!!!

By Catherine Regan, aged 9
Heymann Primary School
EAST MIDLANDS WINNER
NATIONAL WINNER

The Mysterious Treasure

My cellar had become a cave
Full of treasure
Lamborghinis, Ferraris and Bentleys
Such a sight I had never seen

Grand Inventions with huge engines
Long and low to cut through the air
Slick points of red and silver
Coloured bullets of speed

Car keys dangling from the car door
Temptation takes over
A roar, a pant, a snarl and a leap
I'm riding a lion into the night

The deserted motorway of black and white lines
Spreads smoothly away like glass
The thrill of the night
The first drive of my life.

By Joseph Bridgland, aged 9
St Aubyn's School

EAST OF ENGLAND WINNER

The Brownings' New Cat

It was the Brownings' new cat,
But he was not himself at all,
He was wearing pink leather shorts
And a bright orange shawl!

And on top of all that
He was wearing blue boots
And in his ears he wore
Solid gold hoops!

His clothes were just the start
Of this unusual cat,
He began to tap dance
Tap! Tap! Tap! Tap! Tap!

We shut the door
And left it at that
We did not speak again
Of the Brownings' new cat!

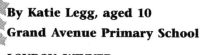

By Katie Legg, aged 10
Grand Avenue Primary School

LONDON WINNER

23

Black Eyes

A place of perfect tranquillity,
Untouched by a human's hand,
For as we stepped through the door,
We knew we were strangers in this land.

Waterfalls spilling like an overflowing cup,
Majestic mountains, secretive trees,
And everywhere around, as far as the eye could see,
Everything and everyone was free.

Manes flying, hooves tearing the turf like a knife,
Bodies straining, eyes wide,
Sleek bodies striving, their trails streaming,
Racing stride by stride.

Eyes searching like a beacon,
Yet eyes without emotion,
Eyes that were as unforgiving as the blackest ocean,
Eyes that were scarred and broken.

We flew on the wings of the wind,
Pictures flashed past us,
The pictures seemed oddly familiar,
As though I'd done it myself.

The horses never stopped,
Never broke stride,
They ran as fast as a cheetah,
Side-by-side.

Now we are in a place of nothing,
No life, no love,
But the horses are staying with us,
Keeping us, watching us, that you can be sure of.

We are at a place where no live being can reach,
And where no one can return.

By Katherine Burdon, aged 10
Bentley Heath C of E Primary School
WEST MIDLANDS WINNER

Weird World

What I saw was a magical sight,
It was a strange view,
I must have made a new discovery,
Now I shall tell you!

There was a lion eating a whale,
And a fish with five eyes,
A wrestler losing to a mouse,
Burgers that taste like fries!

There was a cat acting like a human,
And a squid drowning,
Vultures circling round a live person,
And a pig frowning!

There was a person eating some cola,
A lady drinking pies,
Somebody teething at the age of twelve,
A mole with ten black eyes!

There was a pinky, purpley poodle,
Chickens playing pool,
A dung beetle rolling up the blue grass,
Mice shopping in a mall!

A fully grown lioness with a mane,
A leopard with stripes,
There was a tiger with lots of spots,
And snakes playing bagpipes!

26

Now I have opened this magical door,
And seen secrets behind,
I must now leave this miraculous room,
For someone else to find!

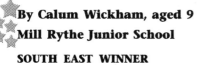
By Calum Wickham, aged 9
Mill Rythe Junior School
SOUTH EAST WINNER

PERSUASIVE WRITING

Nick Arnold wrote . . .

Is Science a GOOD thing?

Scientists try to understand how the world works and answer the curious questions you've always puzzled over, such as "Why is the sky blue?" Their discoveries have made possible every invention you can imagine, from radios to robots. Without the science of forces, electricity and medicine, there would be no roller-coaster rides, computer games or life-saving operations.

"SCIENCE IS GREAT!" I hear you cry. But wait! Some science is horrible too! Without science we wouldn't have to worry about putrid pollution, vicious computer viruses and a host of other nasties. What about cars and planes – are they good or bad?

Thanks to science, humans can blast into space to study the planets and maybe discover new worlds. All that costs loads of money and some people complain that the cash would be better spent cleaning up our own world.

Science can make our Earth a better place – or destroy it. But does that make science our best friend – or our worst enemy?

Introducing the persuasive writing

Science has developed and changed the world. Everything in our lives is affected by it. In his opening piece, **Nick Arnold** asks us to look carefully at the results of science and consider whether they help us or harm us.

Nearly all the winners in this section give examples of how science has improved our world, but they also recognise that it can be destructive. They describe what they feel are the most important advances or harmful effects and clearly express their opinions.

Sophie Wiles asks us whether science is fantastic or horrific. She has used her own experience to support her argument. She also has her own idea for a new invention and challenges scientists to create it!

George Rumney-Kenny's mature and confident piece acknowledges that there are dangers associated with the misuse of scientific inventions, but looks forward to a world that continues to encourage scientists to be creative.

A well-explored and sophisticated argument from **Kate Woodhouse** looks at the pros and cons of science. Her questions to the reader open up her investigations into pollution, cigarettes, drugs, alcohol and medicine.

Paul Scott also believes that we should treat science with caution and never forget that it can have terrible results. He expresses his views clearly and strongly, and asks us a number of direct questions about what sort of world we want to live in.

Chloé Sew Hee strongly believes that science is definitely our friend. She maintains her argument in an articulate style and reminds us of the everyday things we take for granted that are the result of scientific discovery and invention.

In contrast, **Chris Holman's** argument emphasises the negative aspects of some areas of science. This is strong stuff with vivid language creating logical arguments that build up a strong case.

Ben Ward is in no doubt about the benefits of science and his breadth of knowledge and depth of understanding about this topic come through very clearly.

The punchy and amusing style of **Sarah Calvert's** piece aims to persuade the reader that "science is obviously a great thing!" She points out the many benefits of developments in communication, and the power of television to educate and entertain.

Rebecca Worrell's fast-paced piece asks us to consider what a horrible, gloomy world we would live in without science and shows us how modern transport has enabled us to experience other cultures. She uses rhetorical questions to invite agreement.

"What do you think?" **Eileen Stevenson** asks. Her conversational writing style makes the reader imagine that they are having a face to face discussion. She aims to persuade us that science offers us comfort and convenience and has wide-reaching benefits for society.

Science – Friend or Foe?

Is science fantastic or horrific? I have been looking for different but brilliant inventions that have been discovered over the past century to support my argument.

One such modern day miracle was invented by Percy Shaw, who was driving in his car with his lights on in the early 1930s. In the darkness he saw a cat and realised how much their eyes reflected the light. He then went on to invent the reflectors made of plastic and glass which we call catseyes in 1934. They were fitted into the road and nowadays come in a large range of colours. The white ones separate different sides of the road, while red and green catseyes show where you can and cannot go. They show up in even the foggiest of weather conditions and help drivers to see where there are slip roads.

My dad told me that he thinks catseyes are brilliant. "They really show you where you're going and are saving millions of lives every year. I don't know how many more deaths and injuries would have been caused if there weren't any catseyes."

Velcro also is a fantastic invention, discovered by a Swiss mountaineer called George de Mestral in 1948. He was walking his dog and realised how the burrs clung to his clothes. He picked them off and looked at them under a microscope. They had little hooks on them, which stuck to fabric and other similar materials.

Everyone thought this was ridiculous, except for a French

32

weaver at a textile plant. Together they made what they called 'locking tape', which was made from cotton.

However, very complicated equipment and methods were used, so de Mestral searched for an easier way of producing it. Accidentally, George de Mestral discovered that nylon, when sewn under infrared light, formed hooks and the final design was finished.

The only problem left was the name. George de Mestral liked the sound of 'vel' from velvet and 'cro' from the French word crochet, meaning hook. So finally people agreed with Velcro and it is now used worldwide. I certainly couldn't manage to do up laces when I was in the reception class so I always used Velcro trainers. This made changing for PE a lot quicker.

Perhaps one of the most important discoveries of the modern day was made by Sir Alexander Fleming in 1928, at St Mary's Hospital in London. He observed a plate of staphylococcus, which was contaminated by turquoise mould and noticed that colonies of bacteria next to the mould were being dissolved. He was curious, so he grew some more mould in a petri-dish. Fleming found that it produced a substance that killed disease-causing bacteria. He named the substance 'penicillin'. This cures diseases and is still used today.

Howard Florey came to England in 1921 to study. He started to investigate the penicillin mould that Fleming had discovered. He gave mice a dose of penicillin after being fed bacteria and the mice lived.

Penicillin cures lots of diseases and when my mum had tonsillitis she was given several doses of penicillin to make her better and she was soon on her feet again.

I think science is fascinating and brilliant because it can save lives, such as the catseyes and penicillin, whilst other inventions, like Velcro, make everyday life easier. I, personally, would like to see a rug for horses that doesn't slip round and is breathable because horses die because of broken legs and being overheated – horses will be grateful too!

By Sophie Wiles, aged 10
Rookwood School
SOUTH EAST WINNER

Is science good or bad?

I think science is fantastic! Scientists work day and night thinking of new inventions to improve our lives in every way possible. Science is the birth point of nearly every invention or medicine ever thought of, including Marconi's wireless, computers and penicillin. These are all terrific global achievements, benefiting mankind and bringing awe, wonder, surprise and amazement into our lives. In my eyes, science is great!

Microchips are one of the many big advantages for everyone. This little object has made a huge impact on our every day lives. They are in microwaves, mobile phones and my games console, all the time storing information and controlling everything around us. It is often said, that if microchips got into the wrong hands, the world could be destroyed. But, it is not the science that is bad, but the human beings that use it.

Another major advance is the field of communication, which has improved immensely over the last 100 years. Look at Benjamin Franklin's discovery of electricity! Everything has evolved from it. How could we live without it? There would be no warmth, no light and no TV. Into our living rooms, TV brings us news from all around the world. Without it, we wouldn't know about the war in Iraq and we wouldn't have witnessed September 11th; it was as if we were there when it happened. Our homes and lives are made much more comfortable and easier, technology and science combined to great effect. It could be argued that electricity makes us wasteful. Moreover, the use of such energy is contributing to global warming. But surely the benefits outweigh the disadvantages.

Finally, the most fantastic innovations have occurred in medicine in the 20th century. Since Jenner's vaccination, Fleming's penicillin and Hofman's aspirin were introduced, the number of deaths has fallen in huge numbers and we have longer and healthier lives. Improvements in maternity wards mean that there have been more babies that have survived. As a result, there are many, many more people in the world. In response to this there is more demand for the world's resources, such as wood, coal, oil and metal and indeed space. However you cannot blame science or the scientist for progress! We all have a responsibility for the future of the Earth and the quality of our life on it.

So, as you can see from this piece of writing, electricity, microchips and most importantly medicine have all helped us live better and healthier lives. Seeds of ideas grown into wonderful technology to help all of us. Yes, there will be more problems to solve and no doubt we will look to the scientist to find the answers!

By George Rumney-Kenny, aged 10
Leighterton Primary School

SOUTH WEST WINNER
NATIONAL WINNER

Science – Friend or Foe

Science is good and bad and I am going to take this investigation further. As science is such a large subject I could only investigate pollution, cigarettes, drugs and alcohol and medicine.

Look around you. Instead of seeing birds flying past and flowers in full bloom, you see cars zooming past and smoke coming from chimney pots. Both of these things cause pollution. Many other things can cause pollution too, like dumping rubbish into a stream or lake can cause water pollution. But what does science have to do with this I hear you cry. Scientists make some of these awful machines which give off smoke which pollutes our atmosphere. Carbon dioxide is an example of air pollution. Carbon dioxide keeps us warm and without it we'd freeze and with too much we'd boil. Because people are burning fuel with carbon in, it gets dumped in the air, mixed with the oxygen we all breathe and adds to the greenhouse gas problem. What happens next is not good at all for anybody except fish. The north and south poles are melting and at one point all of our oceans will overflow on to land. We will have no place to live, nothing to eat and could die. But there is worse to come. People who study the Earth's climate have found out that as the Earth warms up the weather will get more violent and unpredictable. Hurricanes will become a lot more common which is a big worry for those who live in the United States, in the Pacific and Indian Ocean areas. War causes pollution too, because when a plane takes off it gives off smoke which means pollution, and a fire starts when a bomb lands which means yet more pollution. Many animals die of pollution including the Yangtze river dolphin which has only a few tens in the whole world.

Scientists also have the blame for making nasty things like cigarettes, drugs and alcohol. Smoking can seriously damage your health by giving you lung cancer, heart disease, strokes and bronchitis. Up to 60,000 Americans die each year from secondary smoke (also called passive smoking or sidestream smoke) which is where people breathe in other people's cigarette smoke. Also half of all teenagers who take up the habit will be killed prematurely by it. You could also go blind later in life and your hair could go grey or you may turn bald. When you see somebody lighting up a cigarette they always have a smile on their faces but in just a few years' time they could be in hospital after having a stroke. Drugs are to do with science and so is alcohol. Drugs are often sold on the internet and scientists made that. Alcohol is made by scientists and when you've had too much you may get drunk and the next day you often feel rather sick. Alcohol leads to obesity and death through liver disease.

However one of the good things about science is medicines and cures. Without medicine when you're ill you have to put up with lots of pain and this might make it worse. Some medicines get tested on animals such as cats and dogs which have to suffer by drinking medicine and wearing beauty products for no reason whatsoever. So when you think about it medicine is good and bad at the same time. I disagree with animal testing as I love everything to do with animals. But when I found a discussion board to do with animal testing I found that many people disagree with me and think that we are more important than a tiny animal.

Overall I think that science is a good thing but too many people are using it for the wrong purposes, e.g. profit or power. Scientists should stop working on harmful things such as cigarettes, drugs and alcohol. A more fruitful use of their time would be spent on finding cures for diseases such as AIDS and cancer.

By Kate Woodhouse, aged 9
Ashley Primary School
NORTH EAST WINNER

Shocking Science

Some science is good, but some science is destructive to the Earth such as: explosives, guns and pollution. These are terrible things to destroy our planet.

Acid rain is caused by all the pollution in the air. That could dissolve the natural environment, and destroys animals' homes and their food supplies. It makes birds fly to find new homes while their old homes are burning. Do you want to destroy all the Earth?

Most people think experiments are great for getting things like perfume and lipstick. However unspeakable experiments to make perfume are made on animals and plants that might be dying out. Do you think cruelty to animals is right?

Cars make extremely the worst kind of pollution, because they send terrible fumes out of the exhaust and cause pollution in the air. This is how acid rain is made. Do you want to breathe clean or dirty air?

Many people young and old die innocent, because of explosives and guns. Many soldiers have suffered dying or unexpected injuries. Some people try to stop wars, most are successful, but some can't.

My essay is correct and is proved. You will agree with me and be cautious when it comes to science. Don't think science is all great, because not all science is great. Some kills.

By Paul Scott, aged 10
St Benet's Primary School
IMPROVEMENT AWARDS
JOINT WINNER

Is Science good?

Yes, science is our best friend. It has helped us explore the universe. Because of science we know that there are eight other planets orbiting a huge ball of fire called the sun. Science has also helped us expand our knowledge of the earth.

Science has helped us invent machines like lawnmowers, ovens and fridges that facilitate everyday life.

We then used science to invent cars and planes and trains. These forms of transport are very useful. And yet people argue about pollution. Do they really want to go everywhere by foot? Even long distances? Surely everyone would much prefer hopping into a Mercedes car. Anyway scientists are finding different ways to solve this little pollution problem.

You might still disagree with me and think that science is bad. But wait until you hear this. If astronauts hadn't gone up to the moon computers would not exist. Therefore, there would not be any computer games. Also, science was used to make electronic games. What do you plug the game into so that you can play it? That's right, the television. What was used to invent it? Science. Without science there wouldn't be most of the things we take for granted today.

All this is quite shocking, but the main reason is still to come. What would have happened if we hadn't discovered medicine? Well obviously millions of people would die. Vaccines protect thousands and thousands of people from the most dangerous diseases like measles and mumps. Have you ever had a cold? Your parents most probably gave you some medicine and you would soon be better. If you had a cold before medicine was discovered you could die. Also, long ago the mother could die while giving birth. Now, mothers are less likely to do so.

So, bye-bye quick transport, bye-bye medicine and bye-bye machines. After having reflected on what science has brought us, I have come to a definite conclusion that science is more than good. It's excellent!

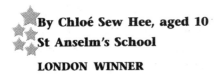

By Chloé Sew Hee, aged 10
St Anselm's School
LONDON WINNER

Is science good or bad?

Science has been around since the dawn of time and, ever since, has solved millions of questions for mankind – but here are some disturbing things about it.

Here are just some of the terrible things about transport invented by science. The pollution made by cars and buses is little by little destroying our ozone layer and poisoning our oxygen. Cars and buses are slowly using fossil fuels but what happens when it all runs out? What about bad drivers? They kill hundreds of people every year and cause thousands of pounds worth of damage. What about unsafe vehicles? They can also kill hundreds of people every year due to faulty parts. The awful thing is most of them are good drivers that just cannot afford to maintain their vehicles.

Now here are the shocking things about science. Medicine can be easily overdosed and will soon make them sick or, even worse, dead. Thousands of people die like this every year because of overindulgence. Also, you can turn a perfectly normal medicine into a deadly drug, which can kill huge amounts of people. The one most annoying thing is when it doesn't do what it says on the packet. However, I defiantly admit that the good things about medicine outweigh the bad, even though there have been terrible things because of science like thalidomide.

Weapons and warfare have been a scourge to our world since man was born. They have, and will, kill millions of people. They became deadly with the invention of the musket and even more deadly with the invention of the gun and now with the atom bomb they are a death wave to all. Here are just some of the appalling things about scientific weaponry. Weapons assassinate thousands every year, which include VIPs, and officials plus other normal people such as President Kennedy. He was killed in his car while it was moving; this shows the advancement in weapons. Also weapons can start huge wars for example, World Wars and Cold Wars. I think weapons are almost certainly the worst things that have happened to the world by far.

Electricity and materials have been all over the world helping, saving, injuring, and killing people wherever they go. I am going to tell you a small amount of the long list of dangerous things about electricity and textiles. Electricity can get so powerful it can leap from telegraph wires, electricity boxes and pylons. There was an incident with three boys who climbed a pylon and electricity leapt from the wires and killed two of them instantly and the other was in intensive care for three months. Now for materials, they can give off toxic fumes that if not stopped will gradually destroy our precious ozone layer and poison our life-giving oxygen. It will wither flowers and turn our rivers into toxic sludge. Electricity can turn perfectly normal objects into a raging fire or overcharge an engine causing a fast joyride to hell. It can instantly destroy anything it touches. Materials suffocate thousands of toddlers and babies every year thanks to the careless use of materials and textiles.

Without science the space shuttle would not have been invented but what about space shuttle Columbia? It killed four innocent people and caused thousands of pounds worth of damage and destruction. The waste made by space shuttles discarding their fuel tanks when they are in space is seriously damaging our atmosphere and will eventually destroy it.

As you can see from my report, science has many failures. It would take only a lone terrorist with a bomb to destroy a whole colony in seconds. So do you think science is good or bad? I certainly think there are life-threatening things about science and the future will be horrible unless we keep a close account of scientific developments.

By Chris Holman, aged 10
Bitterley CE Primary School
WEST MIDLANDS WINNER

SUPER SCIENCE

Everybody knows that science is an absolutely brilliant thing. Without it we wouldn't have marvellous medicine, energising electricity and cool chemistry, to mention but a few sciences.

For one thing, medicine is vitally important. Without it we wouldn't have life-saving operations, vaccines and hospitals. Louis Pasteur (1822–1895) is largely to thank for this. He was the first to develop cures for anthrax and rabies, as well as the process used to kill germs called pasteurisation. He also proved that microbes caused fermentation and disease. Pasteur founded the Institute Pasteur in Paris. He worked there till his death. Another aspect of science in medicine is radionuclide imaging. This involves a radioactive drug being pumped straight to your brain. The drug will stick to a brain tumour and send out gamma rays. These rays are detected by gamma ray detectors to show a radionuclide image of where the tumour is. The drug radiolabelled iodine is hardly radioactive so it does not harm your body at all. Without this technology, many more people would be dying each year. Artificial body parts are another advance in science. Perhaps the most advanced of all these creations is the MO-electric arm. Even with the loss of wrist or hand the sensors in the arm can pick up electrical pulses from the muscles and nerves and move the arm. More artificial body parts include hip joints, heart valves, speech valves and a heart pacemaker. All of this technology makes people's lives considerably longer and less of a burden.

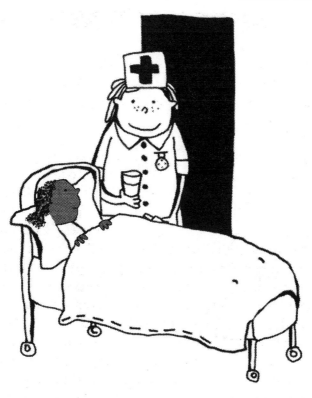

Probably the most important class of science after medicine is electronics. Without electricity we wouldn't have lights, computers, showers and much more. Joseph Wilson Swan was the first to invent the light bulb. Unfortunately, his bulb only lasted for three seconds before blowing. A few years later Thomas Alva Edison improved the bulb. He used charred Japanese bamboo for the filament. He then watched it for 48 hours before deciding that it worked. Nowadays, the filament is made out of metal not charred bamboo. Another great advance in electronics is computers. They can do complex calculations and equations. The making of a computer is very complex. It is made up of lots of computer chips, or integrated circuits. Integrated circuits, or ICs, are wafers of silicon. Each wafer will make around 100 chips. The designs are reproduced onto a photo mask. UV light is then shone through the designs on the photo mask onto a piece of silicon oxide and the silicon oxide is broken down where the UV light falls. Acid is used on the broken down layers to reveal pure silicon. The silicon wafers are then fed into a furnace. More layers are then built up in this way to make a complete integrated circuit. Without ICs no computers would exist. One of the most commonly used functions of a computer is the internet or the world wide web. This is made up of a large amount of web sites. These sites can be viewed by anyone in the world and the sites include homework help, games, downloads, internet shopping and much more. E-mail (electronic mail) is another feature of the web. Anyone can use e-mail as long as they have the right soft-ware. When you send an e-mail it can arrive in New Zealand in seconds. Without electronics our life would be totally different. We would probably still be living in caves.

I have now shown that science is a good thing. Many inventors and scientists have dedicated their lives to science and these discoveries and without them our lives would be totally different. I wouldn't even be typing this now.

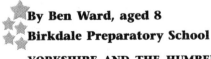
By Ben Ward, aged 8
Birkdale Preparatory School
YORKSHIRE AND THE HUMBER WINNER

Is Science Good?

I think science is truly fabulous! It has made a dramatic impact on our lives.

Electricity is great! In fact I think that it is one of the greatest inventions of all time! Without it we would be using candles as light because there would be no light bulbs. It would be really scary for those people who are frightened of the dark! Imagine life without washing machines! We would be washing all of our dirty things by hand or wearing dirty smelly clothes. We would have to find different ways to entertain ourselves – televisions and radios wouldn't exist and there wouldn't even be as many books as there are now because the fast machines for printing that we have now wouldn't have been made.

The microchip is simply amazing! Without it long journeys would be even more boring than they are now, as there would be no CD players in the car and no television in planes! And more importantly to an awful lot of people, a great number of pets would become lost much more easily. Microchips are implanted in dogs, cats and so on by either an injection or surgical procedure. They are used as a tracking device. Thousands of pets have been reunited with their families thanks to the microchip. Communication would be a lot less advanced as we would have no mobiles, and most children would have nothing to do! No television – not even a computer! Computers rely totally on microchips! All that information on one tiny little chip! Unbelievable!

Television is brilliant! It gives schools educational programmes to show their pupils during lesson time and gives people the opportunity to watch sport matches and live performances in the comfort of their own home. Television can show you what places are like that you aren't very likely to visit. Places like deep down under the sea and on top of mountains – even in the Sahara desert!

Television can help keep small groups or families together watching films or programmes. As well as that it can keep teenagers at home, instead of walking round the streets at night time.

Telephones are excellent! Without them communication would be a lot less advanced. Now, instead of driving round to a friend's house or writing a letter to ask when the disco is, you can just give them a quick call! Very quick and efficient!

Mobile phones are brilliantly handy! When you become separated from a group that you are with you can just make a quick phone call to see where they are!

So, my points show that anyone with a right-minded human brain would know that science is obviously a great thing!

 By Sarah Calvert, aged 10
Crosby-On-Eden School
NORTH WEST WINNER

GOOD OR BAD?

Most people would argue that science is a bad thing because of all the horrid things that might happen. That's not me! I believe that science is a good thing. What would we do without science? There would be no cars, no television and no computers. The sooner you realise that science is a good thing the better. Most right-thinking people believe that science is good.

Computers are a big part of one's life. A faster way of communicating with other people. Ten years ago everyone communicated through letters. Boring! Now thanks to science we can email people. On the internet there are millions of websites which you can visit and learn from as well. Yes in the view of some people the internet is or was dangerous.

Even though some people say mobile phones are bad, I think those people are wrong! Mobile phones are brilliant. About fifteen years ago, you would share one phone between a few other houses. However, now everyone in the family could have their own phone. If you were on your way home from school and your mates asked you to go and play with them, you could easily phone your mum up to change your plans. Could you do that if you didn't have phones? Phones are also great for privacy.

Without medicines what would you do? Millions more people would die every day. Now because of science, less people die each year. If you are poorly then medicines could give you a full recovery. For some people medicines have saved their lives. Every day more and more people go into hospital. However when they enter the hospital they use machines, but guess what scientists invented these machines.

Transport also helps us a lot. Cars can take us from one place to another in hardly any time at all. Without transport what would you do? It would take you about two days to get to London, and even then you would have to go in a horse and carriage. Now with the help of science it takes only one hour to get to London, if you go by train. I don't know what my family would do without science. We would have to walk everywhere. If we didn't have science, we wouldn't have planes and if we didn't have planes we wouldn't have been able to travel from country to country, and if we couldn't go to different countries we wouldn't know anything about people that live there.

So to summarise, I strongly believe that science is a very good thing. If you think science is a good thing then you are a right-thinking person. Without science what would you do? There would be no televisions, no cars, no lights and no medicines. It would be a horrible, dark, gloomy, miserable world. Would you like to live in that type of world? The answer is NO. Now thanks to science we have got a happy bright place to live in.

By Rebecca Worrell, aged 10
Stanwick Primary School
EAST MIDLANDS WINNER

52

Science Wars!

One question that everyone wants to answer is, is science a good or bad thing? Well, coming from my point of view, I think that science has been an outstanding thing that has come to us! I'm very sure that every one of you will agree with me, but I'd like to write down my reasons for why I think science is so brilliant.

Firstly, science has saved us all! We'd be lost without it. Whizz your minds back to when they didn't have this new, modern science. Many people died of illness and diseases. But as we race forward again to about 1900, many more lives than before have been saved because of science. Medicines and professional hospitals are here to help and new drugs are made to cure people's innocent lives. Do you really think that we'd all be here today without science?

My second reason is that science gives us a countless amount of electricity, new machines and helpful gadgets to keep us going. We don't all freeze to death at winter do we? Thanks to the electric blankets, radiators, the hot cups of steaming cocoa. If science hadn't developed in such a fantastically modern way we'd be poor and helpless. We've mentioned winter but what about summer? Whoo do we get hot. But, science has saved us once again and made electric fans to give us air, and think of all the freezers and refrigerators to keep food fresh. Just think what we'd be like without it.

Thirdly, we have transport now! New amazing vehicles to travel in. I know this has to be quicker and better than being trotted along in a cart. When it is a hot day in the car, there is cool air to cool you down and when it's cold there is warm air to warm you up. How convenient is that? Cars have been developed through the years and become better and better. Also, we have many more ways to get around the world. Aeroplanes, ferries, trains. Surely there is more comfortable space in the smallest car than there is in a crummy old horse and cart. Don't you think so?

My fourth reason is that communication with other people has been BRILLIANT with science. Phones have been invented and emails and faxes have been created. This has made it much easier for people to communicate with other people. It is lovely to catch up with your friends and family and I think science has helped us hugely.

Furthermore, science has helped us learn about the world and ourselves. Amazing facts about space have invaded the minds of many and truly lifesaving facts about ourselves have helped us understand how to live. Without science we wouldn't know about the Sun, Moon, Mercury, Venus, Earth, Mars, Jupiter, Saturn, Uranus, Neptune and Pluto. Think how much we have built up in our minds from science.

My sixth reason is that science has given us all these hard-working factories. More food is being displayed in the supermarkets so hungry people can't get enough of anything! Lots of new toys are being made for shops so children can enjoy the games instead of nagging and being a nuisance to their parents or guardians. Brand new furniture is coming and filling our new wonderful-looking living rooms, kitchens and many more rooms.

My seventh and final reason is that we would all be living in caves without science. Science is a word that means lots when it comes to changing all the homes! Instead of living in small caves, we live in houses, flats and bungalows. I am certain this is better than a draughty cave. You have to agree don't you?

So what do you think? If you disagree with me, I do not despise you, but believe that you should think long and hard about what I've just said to you. I know science has bad parts, but do we really think that without the huge step of science, we'd still be where we are now?

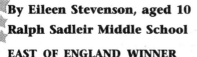 **By Eileen Stevenson, aged 10**
Ralph Sadleir Middle School
EAST OF ENGLAND WINNER

 **STORY**

Gillian Cross wrote . . .

Joss was just falling asleep when Mum knocked on the bedroom door.

"Can I hide Dad's birthday present in your wardrobe?" she whispered.

Joss sat up in bed. "What is it?"

"It's an antique." Mum turned on the light. "Look. Isn't it beautiful?"

She was holding a black leather box. Inside the box, lying on blue velvet, was an old brass telescope. Engraved along one side were the words *Property of Captain Joshua Wright.*

"Wow!" said Joss. "Bet you can see a long way with that!"

Mum grinned. "Hands off! You'll only break it." She put the box into the wardrobe and went out, turning off the light.

Joss lay awake thinking about the telescope. Was it very powerful? Would it let you see hundreds of extra stars? Or things far off in the distance? Surely it wouldn't hurt to take one look?

It was easy to slip silently out of bed and open the wardrobe door. Pulling out the telescope, Joss carried it across to the window and knelt down, resting one end on the windowsill.

There was nothing to see except a few faint stars and a light a long way off. Would it be different with the telescope? Joss leaned forward eagerly, took a long look – and gasped.

"No! No, that's impossible!"

Introducing the stories

Gillian Cross wrote an intriguing story opening offering plenty of potential to imaginative young writers. It certainly inspired the winners in this section to create some unusual characters. Look through the telescopes of these talented young writers and let them tell you their stories.

Joshua Williams' exciting adventure carries the reader along on the crest of the stormy waves. We are thrown into the middle of a battle at sea and Joshua's clever use of language makes the reader gasp for breath!

In **Conor Shrimpton's** story, Joss sees something quite different through the telescope. Excellent attention to detail and descriptive humour really bring the characters and events to life.

Katherine Backler shows wonderful imagination in her original and sophisticated story about a rather special mouse and a magnificent ship.

Joss Marshall's imaginative and inventive story begins as Joss finds himself on board a ghostly ship...what happens to Joss?

The story from **Matthew Goldsworthy** is a real page-turner. He builds tension and suspense when he takes us back in time. But is Joss able to stop certain events happening?

Beth Allison's sinister story introduces a ghost determined to claim back his possessions. The tone becomes more menacing as Joss finds out that this is no ordinary ghost.

In **Anna Emily Corderoy's** exciting story, Joss has a terrifying encounter with a horrific beast which stretches Joss' problem-solving skills to the limit. The excellent use of description takes you right into the story.

The lovely use of language in **Jonathan Douglas'** story mixes fantasy and reality as Joss learns the story behind a group of people in a photograph.

Victoria Barber creates an engaging and sensitive story about how Joss is able to help Captain Joshua Wright.

Annabel Smith builds a sense of suspense in her imaginative story about a space dog. Her detailed descriptions really bring Joss' character to life.

George Wiltshire's well-paced story takes place over a few days, in which Joss realises that the fate of the world is in his hands. Can he act quickly enough to save the world?

Susannah Molisso's inventive story explores the themes of Ancient Greece from a different angle. There is plenty of humour in this imaginative story and the description of the characters is very effective.

The Power of the Eye

"Fire!" CRACK, splinters of wood sprayed Joss' way. A cannonball crashed with the deck.

"Where am I?" Joss asked warily.

"On the HMS Togand," the man said. Joss glanced up. Above him, the man was wearing a pin-stripe uniform. On his hat, in fine golden silk, read "Captain Joshua Wright".

"Take over!" a crew member cried. BANG!

"Good luck boy!" Captain Joshua proclaimed. "Get ready! Fire at will!" he screeched.

Joss got up and automatically, like a robot, went to his position. "Prepare for battle lads, get out your pistols and load them. We are going to board that ship!"

Joss felt scared, he had never killed or attacked anybody in his life. The atmosphere was electric. Joss glanced at the Captain's weapon, it was the rusting brass telescope.

"What are you looking at boy?" he demanded.

"Your weapon, sir, it's a telescope." His voice was a frightened chill.

"It has a built-in sword, look." The blade was steel, perfectly balanced with an aluminium tip. The edge of the tip was a red, dried blood!

"Attack!" The Captain bellowed. "Take no prisoners, only their lives!"

Men were falling by the dozen. Joss felt weak at the knees.

"Aye!" A soldier shouted. Joss, hiding behind a barrel, had been found. He took out his bronze pistol, finger on the trigger.

"Surrender!" Joss cried.

"To a boy," the soldier laughed, "Never!"

Joss' hand felt sweaty, he tightened his grip on the trigger. His heart was racing like a greyhound. His brain was exploding, without any more thought he clinched his eyes together, pointed the gun at the man and pulled the trigger. BANG! The soldier felt his heart, saw blood and fell to the wooden planked deck.

The seas turned into a death trap as a storm blew. The waves were pounding the ship's side as hard as thunder. Already, half of the treasure was lost and the Spanish ship was down at the bottom, gone forever. The conditions were awful, men drowned or died of disease. Joss himself was feeling rather queasy.

Early next morning Joss spotted a second ship so he went to find the Captain. The Captain looked through the rusty telescope, Joss was right. It was coming closer out of the dense mist and fog.

"Prepare for battle lads!" Joshua yelled.

"Boy," the Captain said, "You can stay and look after our ship."

"Aye, sir." Joss replied.

"Guard it we... Ugh!"

"Captain!" Joss cried.

"Doctor, Doctor!" Joss yelled. "The Captain has been shot, will he live?" The sight was horrific, blood was oozing out just like an exploding volcano. Whilst this was happening the dark shape of the ship came closer. The skull and cross bone flag was clear to spot over the horizon.

BANG! The pirates fired the cannon.

"Take cover!" shouted Bill, the second in command. "Load the cannons, Joshua's dead, I'm your new Captain so give me his telescope. Prepare to fight." Everybody raced to their battle stations.

Only Joss knew that Bill shot the Captain. He realised that no pistol or musket could travel that distance or be that accurate.

"Fifteen more minutes until we raid those pirates, they've killed Joshua Wright!" shouted Bill. He went onto the deck, this gave Joss time to put his plan into action.

"Right everyone, Bill is a pirate and a traitor, he killed our beloved Captain. It's time for revenge. Apparently that ship is filled with gunpowder. So when Bill boards the ship then I will throw a torch of fire and he will die."

The ship came closer, the gentle waves washed against the starboard side. Seagulls were echoing their chorus, the pirates' crew were in the hold below.

"Come on lads, quietly, let's board the ship, all together." Bill whispered.

"Captain," Joss queried, "Isn't the Captain meant to board first?"

62

"Ah, yes, fair enough. I'll go first."

Bill boarded the ship. His feet creaked on the boards. Nothing happened. He proceeded until he reached the mast.

"Throw the torch!" Joss bellowed. It launched into the air, it spun vigorously towards the enemy ship. The flame ignited the gunpowder. Joss got knocked backwards and there was a silence.

Joss felt a trickle down his leg. He touched it. It was a cut, it was red, it was blood. It was from a scratch in exactly the same place that he received in the battle. Was his adventure real or was it simply, a dream?

By Joshua Williams, aged 10

Butlers Court School

SOUTH EAST WINNER

Alien Domination

Instead of seeing buildings and the night sky, there hovering over his garden, was a flying saucepan. Joss felt petrified at first but then he thought that the saucepan was a bit strange. He had always thought that UFOs would be more saucer-shaped. But there it was, a saucepan – flashing and spinning over his mum's garden gnomes.

Joss nervously took his eyes away from the telescope. He gasped. The flying saucepan was still there, and what was worse, it looked like it was preparing to land. And it did land, crushing Mum's favourite gnome, the one pushing the wheelbarrow. A huge door burst open and rolled forward like a giant tongue uncurling. A green alien emerged in a little hovering tea cup. Joss wanted to laugh but then he observed the blood-shot eyes, the vicious claws and razor-sharp teeth. Now Joss wanted to run but just then the alien began to speak. His voice was squeaky, like he had been sucking up helium.

"I want my telescope back, you filthy thief. I am Captain Joshua Wright of Spaghetti land and that telescope is vital for my plans for world domination. No one steals from me and survives!"

Hundreds of puny, waddling aliens swarmed out of the saucepan. Each of them carried a laser gun, which they used to blast open the back door. Joss ran downstairs, just in time to witness his parents being transformed into a mound of ice-cubes!

Joss sprinted back to his bedroom and locked the door. He was all alone, except for the scuttling aliens following him up the stairs. Before he had time to think the door exploded open. And Captain Joshua Wright suddenly lunged forwards from the tea cup and tried to snatch the telescope from Joss' hands.

"Men! Arrest that creature!" demanded Captain Joshua Wright.

Thousands of pathetic-looking aliens, brandishing their laser guns, scuttled towards Joss. Before he could even think about taking a deep breath, Joss was overcome with fear. The aliens crawled quickly up his body, just like an army of green ants. Joss felt as if he had been plunged into a vicious nettle bush.

He tried to pick the peculiar creatures off his legs but just as he did so they bit him fiercely on the back of his neck. As soon as he tried to pick the creatures off his neck, he fell to the ground in a flash. He landed in a crumpled mess. Joss tried to pick himself up off the ground but he found he couldn't. It seemed like the creatures' teeth had sucked all his energy out of his body and transferred it into the aliens. The aliens lifted up Joss and took him to the flying saucepan. Just as the aliens stepped onto the tip of the tongue, it began to curl inwards and up towards the door. Inside the flying saucepan the aliens slammed Joss cruelly onto a metal slab. Joss felt the cold. As cold as snow. Suddenly the aliens began to pull out hundreds of blue wires from the control panel which was in the handle of the saucepan. They stuck a few of the wires onto Joss' cheek and the remaining wires they stuck onto themselves. Joss was terrified but he did manage to ask the aliens what the wires were for. They replied, "They help us to study human behaviour. We want to find out all about the telescope. We know you have hidden it in your bedroom."

"What telescope? I haven't got a telescope," he answered.

"Men! Ransack the Alien's bedroom, whatever his name is," demanded Captain Joshua Wright.

"Yes Captain," shouted the aliens.

They shot off into the house like a rocket launching into the air. As they entered the room, they were surrounded by mess. Dirty laundry was scattered all over the room. But despite the mess, they noticed the telescope underneath the window sill. It was still in pristine condition inside the box. They snatched the whole box and scuttled back to the saucepan.

The aliens entered into the saucepan and the Captain shouted with delight, "Excellent! You've got it! Now we can dominate the whole universe!"

Joss lay on the metal slab trembling with fear as he heard the dreadful words of Captain Joshua Wright. It was at that moment that Joss realised he could do no more. His future and that of the rest of the universe was in the hands of Captain Joshua Wright.

By Conor Shrimpton, aged 10
Butlers Court School

IMPROVEMENT AWARDS JOINT WINNER

Mouse Captain

It was a ship! A ship in the sky! A ship, made of stars! Stars!

"Wow!" Joss breathed. The ship sparkled beautifully in the inky darkness.

Then, a quiet, gentle voice spoke. It startled her, as she thought she had been alone. She looked around, wildly, but could not see anyone.

"That's my ship, Joss. Do you like it?" the voice said.

"Where are you?" Joss asked, puzzled. "How do you know my name?" Suddenly, a thought struck her. If he owned the ship . . . "You must be Captain Joshua Wright!"

"Correct, Joss, dear. Do you like my ship?"

Joss then realised who the voice was. It was a black mouse, with detailed white stripes, and a long pink tail. He was sitting on the wardrobe.

"It can't be your ship!" cried Joss. "You're a mouse!"

"Clever girl! I am Joshua Wright, not that rodent."

Joss whipped around and saw a man standing beside the bed. He looked so evil that Joss immediately leaped up and hissed: "Liar!"

Then something very strange happened. The man let out an unearthly scream, and vanished.

"Who was that?" Joss cried, not really expecting a reply.

"That was a doubt. Once he's left us, which he has, your doubt will have left us," replied the mouse.

"Which it has," answered Joss slowly. "But I'd like proof. Not that you're Joshua Wright, I believe that. I'd like proof that it's your ship. Is that possible?"

"Oh, Joss. Of course it's possible," the mouse said to her. "Come with me. I will show you."

Seconds later, Joss found herself standing on the ship she'd seen. It was even more magnificent than she could ever have imagined.

She spent the next few hours exploring the ship. Every nook and cranny, every cabin and corridor she'd explored. Nothing avoided her keen gaze.

Suddenly, a light flashed in front of her. What was it? Then another one flashed, even closer to her. That was when she realised what it was. Lightning. Suddenly, everything went black.

"Joss." She could hear a quiet voice, calling her. "Joss!" There it was again. "Joss, it's me. It's Joshua Wright." Slowly Joss opened her eyes.

"Where am I? What happened? What day is it?" she asked, vaguely.

"You're in your room. You fainted. It's your father's birthday," came the reply.

"What!?" shouted Joss, leaping out of bed. She got dressed in two minutes flat, and raced downstairs.

"Can we start now?" asked Joss' dad, sounding hopeful.

"Yes dear," smiled her mother, fondly raising her eyebrows. So they all sat down, except Joss, who handed a flat, square package to her father, who opened it. It was a CD.

"Wow! Thanks, Joss! These cost loads!" her father told her, and Joss grinned in return. She had emptied her moneybox to pay for the CD, and was delighted to see how much he liked it.

Then her mother presented her gift, while Joss sat down. Her dad opened it, and pulled out the telescope. Sadly, Joss told herself it must all have been a dream. What a brilliant dream though . . .

"Help!"

Her mother was screaming and pointing at a little black mouse with detailed white stripes climbing up the telescope. It hadn't been a dream! Joss leaped forward and retrieved the mouse of the telescope.

Holding the little mouse in her cupped hands, she looked to her father and mother and asked, "Can I keep him?"

"Alright, if you keep him away from Mum."

"Yes, Dad!" Joss grinned, and rushed to her room.

Rattle, rattle, rattle. The wheel in the cage went round and round. Inside it was a small black mouse, with detailed white stripes running all over his body, except for his tail of course, which was long and pink. He loved his wheel, and his cage. The cage was shaped like a large ship, with the wheel as its porthole. On the starboard side was a large wooden sign. Carved into it were five words: Property of Captain Joshua Wright.

By Katherine Backler, aged 10

St Stephen's Junior School

LONDON WINNER

The Property of Captain Joshua Wright

Joss jumped back in surprise and tumbled into the book shelf. It came closer. Joss cowered back and stared straight forward at the huge ship edging towards him. Suddenly, from thin air, a man appeared wearing tatty clothes covered in holes. He was a ghastly blue and his hair was thick with blood. One arm ended in a hook. The other . . . there was no other.

"It calls to us!" he moaned.

"To us-ss!" said another, who appeared by his side.

A sudden red light shot from his eyes and fixed upon the window. To Joss' horror the window opened. But what scared Joss more was that the Captain (or so Joss thought) was clambering onto the edge of the ship, taking a step onto the window sill and stepping into Joss' bedroom. Slowly he reached for Joss and then for the telescope which was on the floor.

"It is ours-ss!" he whispered as he threw Joss aboard and jumped on himself. Joss lifted his head and opened his eyes. He let out a silent gasp and shuddered at the sight of such a gruesome crew. One stepped forward and pulled him to his feet. His body was tall and thin and very bony, but his face was a bashed sphere of ugliness.

"Bow before our Captain!" he growled in a mumbled voice.

The Captain, whose name was a mystery to Joss, stood in front of him looking down at the frightened boy. He held the telescope in his hooked hand with great difficulty.

"What may be your name?"

"Joss," Joss answered in a scared voice.

"And how did you get this telescope?"

"My mum bought it, as a gift for my father for his birthday."

"We are cursed men, Joss! Never to rest until we have found four treasures. A telescope, a medallion, a sword and a compass which were stolen from me and scattered to the four corners of the earth! We have found three. Now we only need the one – the compass. If you help us find it, a reward will be given to you, Joss! Off we are then!" he shouted. And slowly the ship floated away.

"A rest may be a good thing for you, Joss," said the Captain. "A bed you may find down below. Our next meeting will be in the morning!" and he strode off into the night of the ship.

Joss tossed and turned in a damp bunk bed that night. He could not help but think about his troubles. He felt like he was floating away, never to be seen again. Floating, floating nowhere.

He woke up the next morning and stretched. He was lying on sand. He sat up and turned on his bottom to see the Captain and his crew desperately searching for something.

"I can't see it, Captain Joshua!" said one.

"Aha! So that's who he is!" said Joss to himself.

"It was here on the map!" the same man moaned. It was then that Joss sat up straight. He felt around where he had been lying. He felt something hard and cold. He picked it up, and turned it over. It was a compass! Joss squinted at the letters on the wooden case and read out loud "Property of Captain Joshua Wright"!

"I've found it!" Joss called to the Captain. "I've found the compass, Captain Joshua!"

The Captain turned and looked at Joss. He strode over to him. Joss handed over the compass. The Captain turned to his crew.

"Gents, our hope is restored!" he said. There was a loud cheer. "The ceremony will take place tonight. All aboard!"

He turned back to Joss. For the first time Joss noticed something familiar in the Captain's glinting eyes, as if he was looking at his own father! It gave him the strangest feeling he'd ever had.

"What's my reward, Captain?" he said in a suspicious voice.

"Come on board with me and I will give you your reward!"

They strolled up the gangplank and joined the crew on the deck. They climbed up to the bridge and the Captain put his arm around Joss. He shouted in a sudden loud voice, "Raise the anchor, hoist the sails, pull in the gangplank! Your reward, Joss, is to sail the seven seas with Great Great Uncle Joshua and his crew!" He ruffled Joss' hair.

"Great Great Uncle Joshua?" Joss was startled.

"After all, you want to keep up the family tradition, don't you?"

By Joss Marshall, aged 9
Town School

WEST MIDLANDS WINNER

Time Travel

He saw his mum, but she was only about eleven, so that must have been in 1976. He saw the terrible accident that had happened when she was on her way to school with her dad, his grandad. It was a car crash, she was trapped under the car and left with serious injuries. He was scared by what he saw, so he put the telescope back into the wardrobe and went back to bed.

In the morning he got out of bed, got dressed, and went downstairs, still thinking about the events of last night. He stopped at the bottom of the stairs and looked around.

"This isn't my house," he said to himself. He walked into the kitchen. His grandma and grandad were there, but they only looked about 30 years old. There was a young girl there, she looked about eleven and she was getting ready for school. Joss thought she looked familiar.

"Grandma, Grandad," said Joss. They didn't hear him so he shouted louder this time but they still didn't even notice him. Then Joss remembered who the girl was, it was his mum. Joss looked at the calendar. It was the 17th August 1976. He had gone back in time. Then Joss froze, the 17th August, that's the day of the accident.

He had to stop his mum going to school. He wanted to save her from the accident. He ran outside, taking the car keys as he went. He opened the bonnet of the car, and he looked around. Joss didn't know a thing about cars, let alone cars in the past. He opened a lid and found the battery. He took it out and hid it behind the hedge beside the house. He closed the bonnet and watched his mum and grandad come out from behind the wall. They got in the car and tried to start it. The car spluttered.

"Oh, no!" exclaimed Grandad, "the car won't start." He got out and looked under the bonnet. "Someone's stolen the battery," shouted Grandad. "I think I've got a spare in the garage though."

Grandad started to put the battery into the car, so Joss ran as fast as he could to the warehouse where the wagon pulled out and injured his mum. If he didn't stop the accident, his mum would be killed and Joss wouldn't be born.

He tried desperately to think of a way to stop the wagon pulling out on his mum as his mum and grandad turned onto the road. The wagon started its engine, and his mum and grandad drove closer and closer. He still couldn't think of anything to do. He leaned against a wall and felt something cold. He turned round quickly, there was an emergency switch to close the warehouse door. Without any thought he slammed the button and the door raced down just before the wagon pulled out.

His mum and grandad sped past in the car, Joss had saved her. He opened the warehouse door again and the wagon pulled out.

Joss began to spin round and round, he flew up in the air and sped through time and landed back in his bedroom in 2004. He grabbed the telescope and smashed it, bashed it, and he stamped on it, he threw it against the wall, bent it and hit it until it was in hundreds of pieces. He swept it up and threw it as far as he could out of the window.

He fell back on his bed and heard footsteps coming up the stairs. His mum came into his room and said, "What have you been doing? You've been so quiet."

Joss replied, "You don't want to know mum, you don't want to know." Then a thought came into his mind. How can he explain about the telescope . . .

By Matthew Goldsworthy, aged 10
Broadstone Hall Primary School

NORTH WEST WINNER

The Golden Ghost

Joss simply stood there, paralysed with a hurricane of mixed emotions, as the beam of strong, gold light glided nearer and nearer.

When the 'light' reached Joss' bedroom window, she saw that it wasn't a beam of light, but a ghost. Not pearly white and transparent, but pure gold and solid looking.

"W, Who are you?" Joss stuttered, not sure if the ghost could speak.

"I am the ghost of Captain Joshua Wright, and have returned to claim my only remaining possession, my faithful telescope."

Joss remained stunned.

"Your, your only remaining possession?" she asked timidly. "How?"

Captain Joshua Wright surveyed Joss through his light blue, unblinking eyes.

"The rest were destroyed in the shipwreck that claimed my life. They were all lost in the Atlantic Ocean, probably still lying in the depths of it, lost forever. My good friend, Albert, retrieved my telescope in 1920, as I am now. Hand it over, please, Joss." Joss realised her mouth was hanging open, and closed it quickly.

"Hand it over," Joshua repeated.

"No." Joss said simply, but firmly, "It's my Dad's birthday present."

"It's my only remaining possession, please."

"No!" Joss was beginning to get impatient. Why wouldn't he listen?

"OK," agreed Joshua, "I challenge you to a battle. If

you win, you keep the telescope and I will never bother you again; if I win, I keep it, deal?"

Joss agreed reluctantly.

"Hold on."

There was a grin playing at the corners of Joshua's mouth as he said this, which made Joss feel extremely uncomfortable.

Suddenly, Joss found herself lurching forward, spinning as the Captain muttered words under his breath.

Just as hastily as it had begun, the spinning stopped, and Joss found herself in an old, vacated battlefield. She looked around for some sign of Joshua, who appeared momentarily.

"This is where we battle," grinned the ghost, wiping dust from his suit.

"But, where's my weapon?" asked Joss, eyeing the sword that had just appeared in the Captain's hand.

He threw her a sword similar to his, its silver blade gleaming in the twilight.

"And now," he whispered, the grin showing again, "we battle."

It all happened in a blur. Joss, praying that her sword worked against ghosts, fought against Captain Joshua, twisting her sword this way and that.

"Just give in, girl!" Joshua cried an hour later, wiping sweat from his brow.

Joss refused, gave another swipe and, suddenly, a blood-curdling scream pierced the cold, night air. The ghost fell to the ground, once again, dead.

Joss stared and stared at the ghost for what felt like hours, until she felt herself lurching forward once again, spinning until . . .

THUMP!

Joss found herself face down on her bed, listening to the noise of her thumping heart.

Almost at once, the sound of buzzing voices filled the room, spiritual, angry voices, all saying the same.

"We are the Spirits of the dead, your new enemies, because you killed the only golden ghost, we are . . ."

The voices continued, ringing in Joss' ears, poisoning her mind, penetrating her soul. She found herself slipping into blackness, eyes lolling, head drooping, falling, slowly . . .

The end.

By Beth Allison, aged 10
Bill Quay Primary School
NORTH EAST WINNER

The Beast

Joss was horror-struck. His heart was pounding faster than ever. Through the telescope he had seen something . . . unbelievable, impossible. A dark, ruined, haunted house. The walls were crumbling and crooked and the roof was rotting. The windows were shattered and scratched. Some of them were boarded up with decomposing wood. The steps were cracked and a spider's web hung by the door. The faint light Joss had seen was now blinding. The light was coming from inside the house. Joss' mouth was dry and his eyes were watering. As he watched, a dark, purple beast rounded the corner and stood in the doorway. Slowly, it glided out of the house. It was a tall towering figure. It had no body but Joss could make out the outline of a head. The head was covered in a long hood that was shredded and ripped at the bottom. But the worst, most terrifying part of the beast was its eyes. Brilliantly red, they seemed to glare right into his own. As the creature glided closer, Joss began to feel weaker. He soon found he could not see. He could not move either. He opened his mouth to scream but no sound came out. And then, just as suddenly as if a bullet had hit him in the chest, he fell into a crumpled heap on the floor, conscious no more.

Joss' eyes flickered open. He was lying on his bedroom floor, staring at the ceiling. He scrambled to his feet. The atmosphere around him made his insides lurch. The beast was inside his bedroom, gliding smoothly around in the darkness, searching for him. There was a lump in Joss' throat. He felt defeated, like he had just lost the battle. He regretted ever using the telescope. Suddenly the horrific beast turned to face him. Joss stood glued to the spot. The beast's eyes glowed hungrily. There was a long, horrible silence. All Joss could hear was the howling wind outside and the long, slow, steady breaths of the dreaded beast. Joss seized his chance. He jumped sideways onto the soft covers of his bed. He scrabbled to the other side and jumped down onto the hard floor. Without delay, he set off at a sprint towards his bedroom door. This was his only chance. As he reached it, he turned to look back at the beast. A jet of silver light shot from its eyes and hit the solid door. The door glowed pearly white for a moment, then became its normal colour again. Joss leapt for the handle, and tugged. It didn't move an inch. Joss turned and began to scan the room for any signs of help. The beast turned on him. Its eyes glowed red again, just like they had the time he had passed out.

"NO!" Joss gasped. He dodged the terrifying creature and scanned the room again. Something caught his eye. The copper telescope was lying on the windowsill, glinting in the moonlight. And then, a brilliant idea struck Joss. He grabbed the telescope. Now he had to lure the beast to the window. That was the easy part. Once the beast was floating by the window, Joss lifted the telescope to his right eye. He was shaking. He looked, not through the enlarged end, but the shrinking end. The beast turned, and glided out of the window, getting smaller, and smaller. It vanished.

Joss was still shaking. He crossed the room slowly, the treasure of a telescope safely in his grasp. He opened the wardrobe to put it away, when Mum opened the bedroom door. The spell had obviously worn off.

"Sorry," Joss started, "I couldn't help . . ."

His mum interrupted him, "I told you not to use the telescope Joss." She sighed. "IT SAVED MY LIFE!" Joss raged, "I WOULD HAVE DIED! IT SAVED MY . . ."

"All right," Mum spat. "But learn your lesson. Let's put this telescope away."

She walked out of the room and turned off the light. And Joss was relieved. He never put gifts to trial without asking again.

THE END.

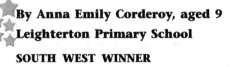

By Anna Emily Corderoy, aged 9
Leighterton Primary School
SOUTH WEST WINNER

The Power of the Wrights

The light was very faint. What he saw nearly made him jump. A one-legged hooligan holding a musket shot pointing at the barman. The old man was holding a jet-black diary stained with blood (BANG!!!). The one-legged hooligan looked past the dead old man, straight into the telescope!!

Joss slept badly. Too soon Dad was opening the jet black box. In the infinitesimal pause before he touched the brass telescope the royal blue velvet slipped and Joss sighted the edge of a photograph. He seized it and pulled . . .

There were three people in the photograph. Two were familiar to him and one wasn't. One elderly man in the top right hand corner had a chunk missing from his ear, also he was wearing a cloak with a hood. Between the folds of his cloak he could just make out the handle of a cutlass and a musket shot. There were two boys, one was Captain Joshua Wright. A badge glinted on his chest. Then there was a knock on the door . . .

Joss reached for the door handle and felt his stomach churn. The man he saw through the telescope was the man in the photograph.

"Give me the telescope," the man croaked, as though his vocal cords had forgotten how to do it. He thrust a diary into Joss' chest, knocking the wind out of him, and grabbed the telescope. He slammed the door so hard that Joss' ears pounded.

The next morning a letter came –

This is the story of how my brother died, Captain Joshua Wright. He went on a mission with 26 men to try and defeat the armies of the Eastern Seas. He didn't know that they had good telescopes too and they saw him coming. They sent 2 galleons armed with 30 men, then they crashed into him and chopped down his sails. Another galleon armed with Gatling guns shot them all down. The traitor is the barman.

P.S. My brother died in a battle and I have struggled to stay happy. Happiness is like a single pane of glass and once it shatters you have to move on and avenge them. I thought I would collect the family goods. Please write back quickly.

Sergeant Chessolodius Wright

Ring, ring. Joss was sitting by the window reading the diary. He went to answer the telephone.

"Hello," a brisk female voice said. "This is Miss Nesbitt. I'm in the middle of a hearing and I would like you to come to it."

"OK."

Half an hour later he was in a long room packed with seats that were filled with people. On a wooden plinth, in a black robe, was the Judge.

"Objection, there is no proof that Mr Wright owns this diary."

"If you give me the diary I will show you that my brother owned it," said Chessolodius. He opened the diary at the first page and read out "John Wright passes down to Joshua Wright," proved Chessolodius, and then he spotted Joss. Joss jumped and looked around, and an old decrepit man took a flat-footed step towards him. He was holding a Bible and beckoned Joss towards him. Joss moved forward apprehensively.

83

The old man asked, "Do you swear to tell the truth, the whole truth, and nothing but the truth?"

Joss replied, "I do," and then sat down to the left of the Judge.

Miss Nesbitt stepped forward and asked, "Did you see a diary through your window on the 22nd of January 1991?"

"All I saw through my Dad's telescope was Chessolodius pointing a gun at a traitor of battle holding a diary, so yes!" replied Joss.

"I have no further questions!" exclaimed Miss Nesbitt.

"I will leave it to the Jury to decide," said the Judge.

The Jury left through a side door. Half an hour later they came back.

"What's your decision?" said the Judge importantly.

"We have decided of his innocence your honour," said the Jury.

"You may take your leave Chessolodius," said the Judge.

Chessolodius left and from that moment Joss didn't hear anything until a letter came. Joss recognised the curly handwriting at once. He opened the envelope with trembling fingers –

Dear Joss,

We have reached the Eastern Shores and will fight our last battle. This may be the last time I write to you.

Your friend,

Chessolodius Wright

Joss wondered for many years. Did Chessolodius die or defeat the armies?

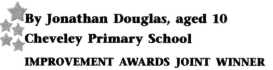

By Jonathan Douglas, aged 10

Cheveley Primary School

IMPROVEMENT AWARDS JOINT WINNER

Captain's Quest

"No, no, that's impossible!" cried Joss as she ran downstairs to tell her mum. When half way down she suddenly realised that she was not meant to touch the telescope. Joss quickly ran back upstairs into her bedroom and closed the door behind her.

Joss froze in fright as slowly she looked up and in front of her was a tall dark stranger holding the telescope. Joss looked at his other hand which was now a hook. Joss was terrified, but as she tried to scream the words did not come out.

"Please don't be scared, I will not harm you," said the man trying to reassure Joss.

"But who are you and why are you here?" stuttered Joss, trying not to appear scared.

"I have only come for the telescope then I will leave, I mean no harm."

Joss was confused. "Why do you want it?" asked Joss.

"My name is Joshua Wright," he began to explain.

"Orrr!" exclaimed Joss, "I know who you are," looking at the name engraved on the telescope. "So it's yours, the telescope it's yours!"

"Yes," answered the man. "Many, many years ago, I was the proud Captain of a ship, but one cold, dark night my ship was hit by terrible storms," explained the man, with a tear in his eye. "My crew fought to save the ship, but there was nothing they could do, everyone drowned in the storm."

Not wanting to frighten Joss any more, the Captain then told her gently how he too had died in the waters, and all he wanted to do was to join his crew and the shipwreck at the bottom of the sea.

"But why do you need the telescope?" Joss asked softly.

"The telescope will guide me back to my ship," answered the Captain sadly, "I will return it back to you before midnight, I promise."

Joss agreed. Now she wasn't scared any more, she felt very sad to hear about all those lives lost at sea.

"Here you are," she said as she handed over the telescope.

"Thank you," said the Captain, "I will not let you down." He then disappeared.

The next morning Joss woke up with a jump. He hadn't kept his promise thought Joss, as she gazed around her bedroom looking for her Dad's birthday present.

She leapt out of bed, and ran to her Mum and Dad's bedroom and pushed open the door.

"Oh Dad I'm so sorry! It was the Captain, he came for the telescope, he said he would bring it back but he didn't," gasped Joss.

"Joss, Joss," said Dad trying to calm her down, "what do you mean?"

"Look in the wardrobe Joss," Mum whispered.

Joss looked in, she couldn't believe her eyes, there it was the old brass telescope the Captain had come back for.

"So he did return it," sighed Joss. "Thank you Captain."

Just then a bright light appeared through the gap in the curtains. Joss ran to the window and peered out of the window. Joss rubbed her eyes, she couldn't believe it, in the distance she could see a tall ship sailing into the morning sun.

"Goodbye Captain," whispered Joss, "safe journey!!"

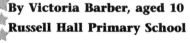**By Victoria Barber, aged 10**

Russell Hall Primary School

YORKSHIRE AND THE HUMBER WINNER

Joss and the Space Dog

A disk-shaped object was heading towards Joss. He strained his eyes to take a closer look. As it came closer, he saw green flashing lights all around it. It was a deep purple colour. Joss flung open the window and leant out, holding on to the wardrobe door for support. Then he spotted it. A flying saucer!

Joss nearly fell out of the window with amazement. He felt cold with fear, as if a bucket of freezing cold water had just been plunged onto his head. The flying saucer suddenly landed in a nearby field. Joss flung on some clothes.

"I'm going to investigate!" he whispered to himself.

The night air was cold. Bits of wind nipped his bare legs. The wind was howling and the moon looked like an evil murderer. The grass and the trees swayed like the seas. Joss walked into the field where the space ship had landed. He saw the space ship much more clearly now as it was on the ground. He lurked down in a bush like a sly cat.

All of a sudden an alien came out of the space ship. It was as purple as the space ship itself, its head as big as a beach ball and its tentacles wriggled as it walked. Its demon eyes glowed like fire. As the alien glided along he left a trail of pink slime. Joss looked and saw the alien was holding something. It threw it in the bush next to Joss. The alien went back in the space ship. Joss didn't dare move. The bush wriggled as it walked towards Joss. Out came a low deep growl.

"Crikey!" he stammered shivering with fear.

He felt if he was being eaten by a monster. The sharks music played in his head. Joss could tell that the thing was big, by the stride of its footsteps.

"What are you? Leave me alone, you don't want me I'm just skin and bone, help, somebody, I'm being eaten!" He closed his eyes and held out one hand trying to protect himself.

He felt a slimy lick on his hand and he heard a small yap. Joss opened his eyes slightly, and saw a green dog, with a big round purple nose. Its tail was short and stumpy with a big yellow ball on the end, its little paws were no bigger than Joss' fingers, its ears were big and pointy and it had five big purple spots on its back. The dog was tiny!

"Where did you come from?" asked Joss. "I need to get you back on the space ship before it takes off!" Joss whispered.

Joss crept down low in the grass like a lion hunting its prey. The little dog bounded after him. All of a sudden a dozen aliens came out of the space ship, setting up tables and chairs. There was food on the table, an eye of a newt, bugs on toast, slug omelette, frog pizza and slime soup. "Yuk!" Joss began to feel sick.

Joss saw something strange, a dog, bigger than Joss, came out of the space ship. Purple all over, with blue eyes and teeth like daggers. Its purple tongue looped over. Its eyes made Joss feel like he would never sleep again! The huge dog came bounding into the long grass. The dog breathed fire! The small dog stepped backwards into the shadows whimpering with terror. Joss turned round and there was the big dog!

His eyes looked like sapphires glowing in the night. A gush of blue fire rushed out of its mouth. It started to chase Joss.

"AAARRH it really is going to eat me!"

Joss saw the little dog standing next to a river. It saw the big dog and scampered away. Joss had an idea. He suddenly stopped but the big dog didn't. It went hurtling into the water. With a splash it landed and didn't come out. Joss went back to a bush and peered over. Joss saw the little dog rush up to the space ship and jump into what he thought was a girl alien's arms.

"Where has my little darling been?" she asked. She was about to walk back into the space ship when the little dog squiggled and came running to Joss. It rubbed its body against his legs and ran back into the space ship.

"I will never forget you!" Joss called after it.

All of a sudden, Joss was back in his bed, the telescope still in his wardrobe. It was all a dream, he thought. Then Joss saw a dog-like figure outside the window. Joss was sure it was a dream, but was it?

By Annabel Smith, aged 9

Kislingbury Primary School

EAST MIDLANDS WINNER

The Ship of Ghosts

For Joss had just seen a ship, or could it have been an oddly shaped star? He had a second look, but he couldn't find it. Just then Joss heard his mother coming up the stairs. He quickly put the telescope back in the cupboard and got into bed until his mother's footsteps passed. He put the telescope back together, but in his hurry he accidentally broke the lens. He quickly put it under his bed and hoped his mum wouldn't notice.

The next day Joss had forgotten all about last night, but as he walked into the living room, with a piece of toast in his mouth, he saw why his whole family was watching the news. "Today on Monday morning news," said the news-reader, "there have been 82 sightings of a UFO in France. Some even claim it was a flying ship, and 20 miles away from the sightings there has been a humungous explosion. A farm has been destroyed and 30 fields with it. Luckily, no one was hurt." The TV showed a picture of what used to be a farm but was now a pile of ashes.

Joss had gone to school thinking about last night and the news report. He knew that there was a ship destroying things and that meant there were pirates on the ship. That night he spent nearly all night preparing it. When he finished he sighed and looked down at the repaired telescope then he thought, why don't I just have another quick look? So he had a quick peek and had a look at a star. It was nothing like what he thought it would be. It had a smooth bottom and a jagged top just like the pirate ship. Hang on, he thought, that is the pirate ship! It was miles nearer than he'd last saw it. It was close enough to read the carved words on the side: Captain Wright's Ship, named the Black Skull. Joss looked away from the telescope and to his surprise he could still see the ship outside the window. Suddenly, there was a loud bang, and Mr McDougal's house had burst into flames, but luckily Mr and Mrs McDougal were on holiday at the time.

The next day Joss knew it must have been something to do with the telescope, and at school the subject never changed at all. All it was was the ship. Because the subject never changed Joss had the night's events fresh in his mind and that was when he thought of how they came to Earth. Joss rushed to the telescope and searched it. Then he found it. Engraved on a lens in tiny writing which read: beware this telescope carries a curse that will roam the Earth forever. Oh but not forever, Joss thought.

That night Joss stayed up all night looking through the telescope until 'check mate' he thought as he saw the ship appear over the white house. Joss acted quickly. He held the telescope in two hands and dropped it on purpose and it smashed into pieces, then he grabbed a modern telescope which he had borrowed from his friend Sid and pointed it at the white house. He saw the ship growing fainter and fainter until it was gone. Joss rejoiced, but just then he thought of the broken telescope. Well, he thought to himself, at least I saved the world.

By George Wiltshire, aged 9
St Paul's C of E Primary School

IMPROVEMENT AWARDS JOINT WINNER

Joss and the Minotaur

He rubbed his eyes and took another look. He could see little flies. No! They were coming closer, Joss saw little people! He strained forward and saw they were flying on little broomsticks! Before he could even think another word, dozens, millions of them were in his room knocking over pictures and whizzing around him.

"STOP!!!" He heard himself scream; at once there was silence, the witches were all huddled inside his wardrobe peering out.

"Who are you? Why are you here?"

One little witch poked her little head out and said proudly, "We are the Tiny Witches!"

There was a little cheer, Joss stood there, and then she said, "But, you see there are also wizards, and whatever you think these wizards are dumb. Their small body comes with an even smaller brain . . ."

There was a small titter from the cupboard.

"And one of them has managed the impossible", she gulped. "He has created the Minotaur! And so we need your help."

Joss nodded taking it all in, in a minute he would be awake in his bed – it would have been a dream. Suddenly a ferocious beast charged through the window, snarling and howling. Joss knew in an instant that this was the beast. It lunged at him; he dodged it and shouted to the witch, "I think we need Theseus!" The witch looked astonished but all the same started chanting:

"To the ancient Athens – without a fuss,
To find the one named These-us!"

Joss stared around him. He was in a palace-type place.

"Now really Theseus, you're risking your life! What if you don't come back, that Minotaur is treacherous!" He heard, it was the voice of King Ageus. Joss grinned, being there in written history!

"Now, now, father! I promise I will return! Look if it makes you feel any better I'll put up white sails if I live and my crew will put up black if I don't. This Minotaur can't keep eating our people; I will finish him once and for all!"

Joss heard ships being moored up, this was his chance. He ran and grabbed Theseus by the arm and heard familiar chanting:

"Back to the year 2004,
Back to rid this land of Minotaur!"

"Where in Athena's name are we?!" cried Theseus.

"This Theseus is my bedroom, and that is the 'modern' Minotaur!" Joss said calmly.

Theseus shook back his head tossing his long golden locks, and with an effortless stab the ugly beast was dead!

"Please can you get that thing off my floor . . . ?"

Joss' sister Henrietta walked in.

95

"JOSS WHAT THE . . . Who is that?" she stared dreamily into Theseus' deep eyes.

"I'm going to be sick!" Joss said cringing. "This is Theseus, you know the Minotaur guy – Theseus this is Henrietta my sister."

"What beauty is before me?" Theseus cried poetically.

Joss felt a tug of his sleeve; it was a little witch! He had totally forgotten that they were there! "Listen Joss, we have to get Theseus back. Oh and Henrietta has to be mind wiped, it would have never worked anyway."

Joss sighed but held Theseus' arm. "Time to go back now . . ." he muttered and the witches cried:

"Now that all is well again,

We save Ageus from ending his reign!"

They were all back at Athens. In the distance a ship (with Theseus aboard) was sailing closer – black sails. Joss understood now, Henrietta was like the woman Theseus had to leave on the island, they would never have lasted – like the witches said . . . so did that mean Henrietta would marry a god?

Suddenly a cry from Ageus was heard. The witches were saying frantically, "Now! Now boy! Run!" A spark or a shot entered Joss' legs making them run faster and faster and even faster! He leapt and held onto Ageus' legs before he could fall, then breathlessly told Ageus, "Look . . . Theseus is on the ship – alive. I've come to save your reign from ending."

Ageus looked quite pale but he got up and said, "May the gods be with you wherever you go. You are strong and brave, you will be written down in history. Goodbye." And with that Joss was in his room with a *Greek Myth* book in his hands. Slowly he turned to the last page which read:

"And so the King was saved by the great and mighty, Joss . . ."

He knew then that the Tiny Witches were home.

By Susannah Molisso, aged 10
St Mary's Prittlewell C of E Primary

EAST OF ENGLAND WINNER
NATIONAL WINNER

⭐ JOURNALISM

Lizo Mzimba wrote . . .

What turns an ordinary report into a great one? Both will tell you the basic facts. What happened, where it happened, how it happened. They might also inform you about things like why it happened. But the key difference is that one just gives you plain information, the other actually makes you feel you were there, and creates a picture in your mind so vivid that it's as if you saw the whole event.

It's the difference between saying "Jonny Wilkinson kicked the ball to score a valuable penalty" and "Crouching in his familiar water-skier pose, Jonny Wilkinson's ever-reliable boot brought England three points closer to their dream."

Here's another example. If you're writing a TV report on a big film event you could say "At the premiere the crowd screamed loudly when J K Rowling appeared." But that's vastly different to "The loudest cheers were reserved for the muggle behind the magic of Harry Potter, J K Rowling, with the crowd's screams louder than at any Quidditch World Cup Final."

In both cases, the second sentence helps you understand much more easily what it was like being there.

Children were asked, in groups, to choose one of these pictures and to write a TV report or newspaper article about it.

Introducing the journalism

Lizo Mzimba suggested that good report writing helps readers to feel they were there to experience the event for themselves. This is exactly what the winners did in their reports, creating powerful written images of some unusual events inspired by the three stimulus pictures.

In their Newsflash, the young TV reporters of the **Croft C of E Primary School** show tremendous appreciation of modern TV news and the language and humour make the report feel really believable.

The budding sports writers at **Hardwick Primary School** give us a very realistic piece of reporting as they describe the build-up to the final of a football championship.

The clever alliteration in the headline to **Burford School's** team of reporters – *Big Ben's Blown Beyond Birmingham*! – opens their TV piece on freak weather conditions. The reporting style is very realistic and the good use of imagery keeps you on the edge of your seat.

The journalists at **Priory CE VA Primary School** issue a strong warning to the public not to approach escaped zoo animals. The reader is even told what to do if they see a tiger!

The realistic live sports programme from **Dunningford Primary School** is very witty and funny. The reader is

taken to Madrid to hear the report of a football match that ends in an unexpected way.

An eye-catching headline draws us into this inventive and witty article by the local reporters at **Tany's Dell County Primary School**. This is a well-written report about some remarkable animal behaviour.

Another clever headline brings us the scoop from **St Patrick's Catholic School** about the effects of the windy weather and engages the reader immediately with its lively style and imaginative descriptions.

The reporters from **Portway Junior School** are out on the streets of Housington helping TV viewers to experience the events when some animals escape from the local zoo. It is humourous and has a lively style.

St Winefride's Catholic Primary School's report *Euro 04 Dead as a Dodo*? is an amusing and well structured piece of journalism on the year's big event in football. But what happens on the day of the final is extraordinary!

Newsflash

Lizzy: Welcome to Newsflash. We've had reports just in that some animals have escaped from Oxford Zoo, but the number has not yet been confirmed. I'll now pass you over to Martin who's live at the scene with more information.

Martin: Thanks Lizzy. Now, this incident took place this morning when the zookeepers were cleaning out the cages. One of the apprentice zookeepers Edward Boyes was putting the animals in their temporary cages and was supposed to be locking them. Unfortunately he forgot to lock them, but only 3 animals managed to escape before the head keeper went to feed them and found the cages unlocked. I'll pass you over to Jim who is interviewing a shopkeeper, Katie Bearpark, who got a shock when she saw a penguin outside her shop.

Jim: Thank you Martin. I'm here with Katie Bearpark the owner of the local shop. How did you feel when you saw the penguin?

Katie: I was like really shocked you know what I mean, I don't think I've ever seen a penguin in the street before.

Jim: Do you feel it has driven any of your customers away?

Katie: I think I only get about forty customers a day so it probably drove a few away, but the ones who do come are buying a lot more birdseed!

Jim: What did you do when you saw it?

Katie: Well at first I tried to shoo it away, but it bit me hand then it tried to follow me into the shop when I went to get the first aid kit, so I called the RSPCA who came and took it away. I think they took it to the zoo. I can't really remember.

Jim: Thank you Katie. Hope your hand gets better soon.

Lizzy: Have you any advice for the people watching at home?

Jim: Yes I do actually. If you do come across an animal that you've seen in a zoo, especially a tiger or a zebra, please contact a member of Oxford Zoo. Also try to avoid roadblocks on Green Lane and on part of the A1685 as this is the area where the animals have been sighted. Now over to Kirsty who is down in Merton in London interviewing Doctor Nicholas Turner, the most senior vet in England.

Kirsty: Cheers Jim. As Jim has already said this is Doctor Nicholas Turner. Now Doctor Turner, do you think that the animals were in good condition and being well cared for?

Doctor: We have monitored the zoo for some time and tested the animals; we have found their care has not been up to standard.

Kirsty: I hear that people have been protesting against the zoo's dreadful conditions. Are the conditions actually that bad?

Doctor: The conditions the animals have been left in are terrible, for example lion carcasses have been found knee deep in manure so I can see why the animals ran away, but they are now trying to improve the conditions and see a smile on visitors' faces.

Kirsty: Do you think the penguin will survive outside the zoo?

Doctor: It will survive for at least a week if it has a good supply of water; if it doesn't it will only live for about another five hours, so we are trying to direct it to water. As this is one of the only male Emperor penguins in the zoo's breeding programme we are very concerned.

Kirsty: All we've talked about is Chilly the penguin, what about the other two animals?

Doctor: Well we've caught Sparky the zebra grazing in a park and Prowler the tiger was found trapped in a skip and we are currently trying to free him by sedating him and moving the blocks around him, but as he is only young we can only give 20 minutes of

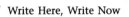

drugs every hour and the job will take at least three quarters of an hour.

Kirsty: Thanks Doctor for an interesting talk. We hope you are successful. Now, back to the studio with Lizzy.

Lizzy: If you'd like to find out more details and information on the zoo crisis at Oxford, log on to our website at www.croftschool.com/newsflash. That's it for now but to find out more exciting news stories tune into us at noon.

By Mark Millman, Simon Walton, Lydia Armstrong, Harry Evans and Jenny Young, aged 10

Croft C of E Primary School

YORKSHIRE AND THE HUMBER WINNERS

Red Arrows Rise Again

Reporters: Thomas Squires, Damian Burr, Jack Buckle and Sam Stokes

On Wednesday 13th February at 7pm the semi-final of the Old English football tournament took place at the Red Arrow Arena.

There was a tense atmosphere in the Arena as the Red Arrows entered the Arena with their opponents, the double winners, The Black Foxes. The capacity home crowd cheered, as both teams lined up on the pitch.

In the first half Eamon Kellap, the Red Arrow's left midfielder, took a corner and the crowd groaned as Luis Corral hit the crossbar. Frankie Kellap powered the rebound shot towards the goal. The Black Foxes all star Russian keeper, Simon Pavlov, made an excellent save on the line.

In the second half it was 0–0 until the 89th minute when just as the dissatisfied fans were leaving, the Red Arrows gained a dangerous free kick. Jay-Jay Jackson took the free kick from his usual position, just on the edge of the box. He blasted it into the back of the net and took them one step closer to their dream, a place in the final.

Jay-Jay Jackson scores the winning goal

We interviewed Jay-Jay Jackson in the dressing room and we asked him what it was like to score a winning goal. He said: "It was wonderful, the best time of my life! We can't wait to play the Green Rabbits, even though we know it will be a challenging match."

The final of the Old English Cup is on Sunday at 2.30pm at the Green Burrow. Tickets are still available at the ground.

By Jack Buckle, Thomas Squires, Damian Burr and Sam Stokes, aged 10

Hardwick Primary School

NORTH EAST WINNERS

Big Ben's Blown Beyond Birmingham!

"Good evening and welcome to the ITV News at Six with Ellis Bell. We have some breaking news. Over to our special correspondent, Toby Aldred with the latest . . ."

"For the first time ever in this country a tornado, the size of a fully-grown T-rex, hits London. Time is flying by – Big Ben has been taken from London's streets by the menacing tornado. Big Ben is flying high, chaos for London, people screaming for shelter, animals fleeing in fear. The tornado has already taken down two hundred and seventeen houses, one block of flats and an office. I'm standing where Big Ben stood. Over to Tom."

"Thank you Toby. The storm is rapidly growing. Some people in Birmingham have never seen Big Ben before but now they can see it flying past their bedroom window. A ten-year-old boy staying here with his aunt remarks that this is the worst thing that has happened in his life so far. The tornado is turning round and is heading towards Marlow in Buckinghamshire."

"We'll see you after the break."

"Hello again and now back to Tom in central Birmingham."

"Thank you, Ellis. The storm has now left Birmingham. People are relieved that the storm is gone and they are safe, for now. The amazing thing is, it's mid-summer here in England, and there is a white blanket covering Birmingham. The rivers are frozen, snowflakes are falling and the temperature is below freezing point. I think we should see what's happening in Buckinghamshire. Over to Scott . . ."

"Thank you, Tom. We can see the tornado in the distance, so I advise everyone to stay in their houses. The tornado's location is now Oxford and is getting nearer every second. People are driving down to Cornwall, as fast as they can, but those who don't have cars are running for their lives. Some people are even driving to London and hiding in the underground stations, for shelter. Back to Toby at Chiswick Park underground station."

"Thank you Scott, as you can see the underground station is packed with people, who are so desperate for shelter, they are even standing on the train track and holding onto strong metal bars so they don't blow away. I'm just moving down to the track to see what it's like. People are running as far down the tunnels as they can go, because more people are coming into the station as we speak. The trains are closed and people are speeding down the motorway to find places with shelter. People with basements are advised to hide there."

"Thank you Toby we'll see you after the break."

"Back to Toby in London."

"Thank you Ellis, according to satellites the tornado is heading down to Cornwall. Scott is driving down to Cornwall as we speak. Over to Scott . . ."

"I'm driving down to Cornwall. We can see the tornado. It's getting nearer to the motorway. Oh, my gosh! The tornado has just crossed the A30, and has taken at least ten cars off the road! I'll see you back in Cornwall after the break."

"Hello again. Here in Cornwall people have set up tents on any patch of grass they can find. But tents won't be any good, because the tornado has cornered us here down in Cornwall. Wait – the tornado is changing course . . . and is heading towards the ocean. It's dying out! It looks as if the tornado is going to die out completely in the middle of the ocean!"

"Everyone in the country is celebrating that the tornado is gone."

"Thank you for watching the ITV News at Six."

By Ellis Bell, Scott Pimlott and Toby Aldred, aged 9, and Tom Fulford, aged 10
Burford School
SOUTH EAST WINNERS

Terrible Tiger Trauma
Reporters: Miss N Steel and Miss S Rolt

A tiger and a penguin have escaped from the zoo. It happened yesterday at 14.30pm and the zoo-keepers have been looking for them since. Read on to find out more . . .

London Zoo has lost a penguin and a tiger that are either on the street or in someone's home.

Zookeeper, Sophie Hulbert, age 35, announced yesterday, "The tiger had been named the most vicious in all of Britain and if it is let loose, who knows what damage it could cause!"

The tiger has already caused great damage. A pupil, Rachel Pilley, age 10, has experienced what it is like to be savagely attacked by one of the world's fiercest tigers.

When asked she said "I was just walking down to the park when I saw the tiger. I had heard one had escaped from the zoo but it didn't worry me since I was quite capable of taking it back to the zoo. Well that's what I thought but I was a bit wrong and instead of taming it, I got my left leg bit off. I was straight away rushed to hospital."

Everyone in London is in great danger, that tiger could seriously injure someone. So keep all your doors securely locked and windows tightly shut.

The penguin has been found safe but the tiger is still on the loose. If you see the tiger call the zoo immediately. Be on the lookout at all times.

112

By Natalie Steel and Symmi Rolt, aged 10

Priory CE VA Primary School

SOUTH WEST WINNERS

News Report

Allesandro: Hello and welcome to Champions News with me, Allessandro Moore in Spain where a phenomenon has taken place at the Bernabéu stadium. David Ugueaunea (known as Useless Ugueaunea) has won the UEFA champions league for Real Madrid fourth time running. Over to you Sucheenoh.

Sucheenoh: Hi, Allessandro, yes, the fans are stunned to silence here in Madrid! They are ecstatic after Real Madrid's last minute winner by David Ugueaunea. David (number 65) has been scorned all season for being a walking disaster. He was bought from Canvey Island for £2.50 with a free football and first aid kit thrown in. Real Madrid needed an extra player or they wouldn't have been able to play as their key striker, Ronaldo, is on loan to Chelsea. Back to you Allesandro.

Allesandro: Well we ought to overlook the highlights of the absorbing match so let's join Justin Annette for a run-down on events.

Justin Annette: Yes, hello. Today's magnificent game started as Ronaldinho headed home after just ten minutes. Twenty-seven minutes later the same super striker scored another goal to make it 2–0 and on the stroke of half time Edgar Davids made it 3–0 from the edge of the area. Madrid fans were devastated by this crisis at half time. It really didn't look good for them.

The second half kicked off and Roberto Carlos thumped the ball down the field to Petersen on the wing, who crossed it in and Adye-Curran dive-headered the ball past the keeper and in the goal. This took the score to 3–1. Then shortly after, Petersen shot from forty-two yards. The ball hit the underside of the cross bar at an amazing pace and spun in the net making it 3–2. Ten minutes from full time Zidane was taken down by Cocu just outside the area. Sickelmore stepped up and curled the ball magnificently over the wall and in the top corner of the net: 3–3. The title was there for the taking.

The clock was ticking with 87 minutes gone, when suddenly, Raul was thrown to the floor and injured by Eddie Elbower. David Ugueaunea (Useless Ugueaunea to the fans) came on for him to terrible chanting from Madrid supporters. The next 3 minutes were the most miraculous in football history with Madrid desperate for a winning goal. Sickelmore passed the ball along the ground to Petersen who chipped the ball over to Adye-Curran. He then volleyed it across the penalty area to Ugueaunea who turned around in fear and started to run away in the opposite direction. However, he tripped over his shoelaces, the ball hit him hard on the buttocks and span into the goal like a rocket to the surprise of the startled keeper. The final score was Barcelona 3 – Real Madrid 4.

Allesandro: So you could say bottoms up then.

Justin
Annette: Yes you could.

Allesandro: Let's hand over to George Kick.

George Kick: I have here with me some of the stars from that brilliant game. Hello Useless Ugueaunea, sorry, I mean David. How did it feel to score the winning goal?

David Ugueaunea: Brilliant George. Yes I am pleased I scored. I showed those people how well I can play, and I see my career going very far . . . ummnnn . . . got any Deep Heat spray for burns?

Allesandro: Sorry Ugueaunea. Still, no pain, no gain! That's all from us folks. Thanks for watching Champions News. Goodbye from me and everyone here in Spain. Good night.

**By Scott Sickelmore, Jaime Petersen and
Keith Adye-Curran, aged 10
Dunningford Primary School**

LONDON WINNERS

TIGER TERRORISES TIPTREE!

Yesterday 16th June a most shocking sight in Tiptree horrified local citizens. They were terrified to see that one of Colchester Zoo's Bengal tigers had escaped along with an innocent penguin. Mr Bill Briggs, the zookeeper, made the discovery when he went to feed the tiger at midday and he was then informed that one of the penguins was also missing. After alerting the emergency service Mr Briggs left the zoo with his tranquilliser gun and net and made his way to Colin's Convenience Store, where the two escapees had been spotted by a member of the public.

Our reporter Rebecca Reynolds went to the scene and spoke to some of the people who were affected by this event. A young woman with her baby had this to say, "I was going to the shop to get some milk and there in front of us was a great big tiger and a cute little penguin, I couldn't believe my eyes, I thought I'd walked onto a film set, but then the zookeeper appeared and shot a dart at the tiger and it fell to the ground, it was very upsetting."

Rebecca also came across a group of school children who had just been on a trip, some of them were still screaming while others were sobbing uncontrollably. Ten year old Vanessa Anderson said shakily, "I was petrified and started screaming. I thought that it would kill us, my teacher told me to stay calm but how could we when there was a killing beast on the loose?"

The local police inspector made this statement, "The zoo alerted us as soon as the disappearance was noticed, we immediately swung into action. We interrupted local radio and TV advising people to stay in their homes until the danger had passed, we also sent loudspeaker cars out around the town asking people to clear the streets. We have never had to deal with this sort of emergency before but everything went very well, there were no injuries to anyone and the tiger and penguin are now safely back behind bars where they belong."

Back at the zoo Mr Bill Briggs was still clearly upset and he had this to say, "This is the first time anything like this has happened and we are going to investigate how both these animals managed to escape at the same time. The penguins are free to run around the area where their water is as they pose no danger to anyone, but the tigers' cage should be securely locked at all times. A witness has come forward and has told us that he saw a penguin near the tigers' enclosure and it looked like it was beckoning the tiger to follow him as the gate seemed to be unlocked, this is of course ridiculous."

Rebecca Reynolds thought this sounded interesting and decided to investigate further. She contacted the well-known animal behaviourist Professor Adams and asked him if it was possible for a penguin to be unafraid of a tiger and for it to seem to be encouraging it to escape.

Professor Adams replied, "Strange as it may appear, I have known these sorts of friendships in the animal kingdom before. You must realise that penguins are very clever and tigers although appearing to be fierce are easily led astray and I believe that this is what happened in this case. This was no innocent penguin threatened by an evil tiger, but a stupid tiger being used by a very bright but crafty penguin."

The whole of Tiptree is relieved that both animals have been safely returned to the zoo without any harm coming to either of them or to any of the residents of the town.

By Katie Henderson, Taylor Howard, George Stokes and Ben Randall, aged 10, and Jamie Morley and Connor Thorogood, aged 9

Tany's Dell County Primary School

EAST OF ENGLAND WINNERS
NATIONAL WINNERS

Stafford Scoop
WINDY DAY TAKES BREATH AWAY!!!
Stafford is stolen . . . by strong wind!!
Reported by Kate Harvey and Phoebe Dale-Parry

Stafford is stunned
Yesterday, Stafford had a shock when gale-force winds hit their town suddenly.

This monstrosity first hit Rowley Park, when St Patrick's Catholic Primary School was trying out for the school's running race. The atmosphere was tense, but as they crossed the line for the first lap, trees blocked the track, and children were running from the freak hurricane. Some children came back home with broken bones, as the wind was so harsh. Some children who were racing tell us about the chaos.

"I was just doing my long-jump event, when a massive gust of wind blew me right over, with the sand thrust in my face." exclaimed 10-year-old Nicola, who is now recovering from a sprained wrist and a bad eye. 9-year-old Ellie Miller reported, "There was so much pandemonium, when I was practising my sprinting, chaotic wind took my breath away, and left me stunned."

Where is it now?
The wind was identified as a small hurricane, and left Rowley Park in a state, and by now, had hit Stafford town centre. The wind had swept up most of Stafford, and the weather forecast had not given any clue about a hurricane, as people were out having picnics in the Town Park,

when sandwiches were blown up into the sky, and crisps were scattered. The citizens accepted the forecast as a sunny, bright day but soon got a shock, as the sky ate their picnics.

play park will cost a whopping £3,000! Bob, one of the builders said to us, "I can't believe how much damage has been caused, it is shocking what this wind has done, it will take

The damage

Because of this horrific, shocking incident, a lot of damage has been caused to Stafford. The biggest mishap was that a third of Rowley Park play area had been blown over, and as far as builders and firemen are concerned, to rebuild the

weeks, even months to renew Stafford."

Now's where you come in! If you spot this hurricane, or you spot any more damage, please call us, or the police on 999, so we can take drastic action!

By Kate Harvey and Phoebe Dale-Parry, aged 10
St Patrick's Catholic Primary School

WEST MIDLANDS WINNERS

Animals Patrolling the Streets

Zoë: Hello and welcome to Newsround, I'm Zoë Clark and our main story today is the animals from Housington Zoo have escaped.

Disaster struck early evening on the 20th June when the zookeeper forgot to lock the gates of the penguins' cage, the snakes' hut and the crocodiles' pen. As soon as the zookeeper had gone the animals began to creep out of their cages and on to the dark streets of Housington. In the past 50 years none of the zookeepers before have ever left the gates open of any cages.

We will now go over to Katy who is with Rory the zookeeper. Over to Katy.

Katy: Thanks Zoë, I'm here with Rory Jackson the zookeeper. Rory, are you afraid that the animals on the streets could cause danger to the innocent lives at risk?

Rory: Yes, they could be very dangerous.

Katy: How do you think you will catch the animals?

Rory: We're not sure what our next move is but we will definitely try to put them back where they belong.

Katy: Good luck finding them, now back to Zoë in the studio.

Zoë: Thanks Katy, another disaster was when all the penguins went into the fish and chip shop. Mark is there now with the full story.

Mark: Thanks Zoë, it's a devastating scene here in the local fish and chip shop of Housington, the glass is smashed and the deep fat fryers have been set alight by a swarm of penguins on the loose looking for fish. Amazingly they haven't touched a single chip. Here next to me is Dr Hudson of the Housington health and safety organisation, who was surveying the building at the time the penguins came in. Dr Hudson, do you really think this is hygienic?

Dr Hudson: No, not at all! The penguins could have picked up a disease on the way here or something like that.

Mark: Are you going to close the chip shop down?

Dr Hudson: Of course I am. A disease that's come off one of the penguins could still be on the surfaces and stay there for months.

Mark: Thank you for that update. Now back to Zoë.

Zoë: Thanks Mark for that shocking story. The snakes went out of control as soon as the gates were open. They slithered straight out to Cook Close where they are patrolling the streets at this moment. Now let's join Emma who is with local citizen, Betty Bosworth.

Emma: Thanks Zoë. Hi, I'm Emma Lake and I'm here in the quiet town of Housington, at number 42 Cook Close. And here next to me is Betty Bosworth. So Betty are you afraid to come out of your house because of the snake?

Betty: Well I am scared, but I suppose I can't stay in my house forever!

Emma: Were you scared when you first heard about the snakes being on the streets?

Betty: Yes I was, because I have never been near a snake apart from seeing a few on TV.

Emma: Okay thanks for your time Betty. Now it's back to Zoë in the studio.

Zoë: Thanks for that amazing story Emma. We will now go over to Liam with the latest news about a crocodile in the local swimming pool.

Liam: Thanks Zoë. I'm here interviewing Lauren the lifeguard at Redsworth swimming pool. So Lauren were you shocked to discover a crocodile in the pool?

Lauren: Yes it was an awful shock to notice the crocodile in the pool.

Liam: How are you going to get the crocodile out of the pool?

Lauren: We have decided to leave that to the Housington Animal Rescue Association as we do not want to hurt the crocodile or ourselves.

Liam: Thanks Lauren. Now let's hand it back to Zoë in the studio.

Zoë: That's all for now but join us tomorrow for some more amazing headlines and updates. Goodbye for now.

By Hannah Jones and Kurt Lakin, aged 10, and Daniel O'Key and Joanna Lambourne, aged 9 Portway Junior School

EAST MIDLANDS WINNERS

Newspaper Report
EURO 04 DEAD AS A DODO?

On Sunday, 4th July, the Final of Euro 2004 was cancelled, owing to a flock of dodos interrupting the Portugal v Greece game, held at the Stadium of Light, Lisbon. Nathan Gomales has been injured. All the players are horrified.

In the last minute of extra time, Portugal captain Lorenzo Fuez was about to take the penalty to decide the champions of Euro 04, when suddenly he heard a wild flapping noise above his head. He looked up and saw a large flock of strange birds forming a triangle shape. They were dodos!

The dodos landed on the pitch and then took off, ripping and tearing at Nathan Gomales. They badly injured his right foot. Then they got hold of the ball and began whacking it on his head. He is still knocked out in Acha Hospital, Lisbon, but his family is eagerly waiting beside his bed.

Lorenzo Fuez said, "At first I didn't realise what they were, I hadn't seen them before. My dad and I used to go bird watching every Sunday and we never saw that kind of bird. I only knew they were dodos when a young Portuguese fan, aged about ten, recognised the birds were off *Ice Age*. He shouted, "Hey they're dodos! They're meant to be extinct!" Then the crowd went wild. When Nathan Gomales got knocked out I got scared at what they could do and ran into the changing rooms."

One of our reporters interviewed a policewoman,

who told us that the fans were wild but behaved better than she expected. She said, "I was a bit scared of the dodos but they didn't come near me. Some of the other police-men tried to stop the birds, but none of them succeeded."

Professor Jay Cuttler, a scientist who studied the dodo at university,

explained that dodos belonged to the order Columbiformes, and were as large as a turkey with short curly feathers, big beaks and big feet. They were exterminated by early settlers around 1687. "Dodos aren't very clever and sometimes don't realise what they're doing," he told us. "We hope we can catch all of them and try to find out more about them, taking DNA samples from their feathers to see if they're the same as the extinct ones. What is most amazing is that dodos have never been able to fly!"

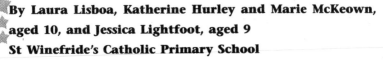

By Laura Lisboa, Katherine Hurley and Marie McKeown, aged 10, and Jessica Lightfoot, aged 9
St Winefride's Catholic Primary School

NORTH WEST WINNERS